Pasta Fazool for the Wiseguy's Soul

D171443ь

Pasta Fazool for the Wiseguy's Soul

Heartwarming Stories of "Family" Life

(A Parody)

Brian M. Thomsen,
as told to him by Don Minestrone

**Andrews McMeel
Publishing, LLC**

Kansas City

08 09 10 11 12 RR2 10 9 8 7 6 5 4 3 2 1

ISBN-13: 978-0-7407-7230-6
ISBN-10: 0-7407-7230-9

Library of Congress Control Number: 2007934894

www.andrewsmcmeel.com

For Frank Weimann
A regular guy and a wise man
(y'know, an all-around goodfella).

Contents

Introduction

I had been away from New York for a while.

The business of publishing had required me to move out of state for a few years when I accepted a position running a book division (and later a magazine division, as well) for a prosperous Wisconsin-based corporation.

Now, don't get me wrong. The Midwest was great. The people were friendly. The weather fine for anyone born with north-of-the-Mason-Dixon blood. And the beer, cheese, and football were without parallel to any other location.

But it just wasn't Brooklyn.

So when the opportunity to return presented itself, back to the borough of Kings was I bound.

Back to the home of Greenwood Cemetery and New Corners restaurant.

Back to the borough that gave us Woody Allen and Mel Brooks, Pat Benatar and Barbara Boxer, Al Capone and Alan Dershowitz, Rudy Giuliani and Joey Gallo, Lena Horne and Spike Lee, Vince Lombardi and Norman Mailer, Bugsy Siegel and Beverly Sills . . . well, you get the idea.

Now, one of the things I missed most about Brooklyn was real Italian restaurants—not Olive Garden or some upscale pizzeria, but rather the spacious family-style restaurant with the huge, oversized menu that was perfect for a "no one wants to cook" night or a family occasion of celebration or solidarity, as well as the hole-in-the-wall, twelve-table establishment that always seemed to have the table in the corner occupied by two or more guys talking over plates of pasta.

It was in the latter of these types of places that I first made the acquaintance of a man whom I will refer to as Don Minestrone (for that was the only name he gave me).

Having just handed in a book to a publisher, I decided to treat myself to a reasonably priced treat of spaghetti and meatballs.

The lunch crowd had passed (or at least what passed for it in this part of Brooklyn), so I settled in to enjoy my meal.

There were as many people working in the restaurant as there were customers, and no one seemed to mind.

Two businessmen were finishing their aperitifs at one table and a young couple were arguing at another and in the corner was an old man nursing a bowl of pasta and beans.

Now, this old guy looked just like what you imagine a retired don would look like—sort of like the kindly old gentleman depicted on the label of a bottle of Moretti beer, and he really seemed to be enjoying his meal, savoring each spoonful.

After I had placed my order with the waiter, I began to have second thoughts and inquired of the server as to what the old gentlemen was having . . . and he was about to answer me when the rudeness that the young couple had served to each other began to overflow as they shared it with the server in the form of complaints too numerous to take seriously.

"Pasta fazool," I heard from the opposite direction.

"Excuse me?" I said, directing my attention.

"You were going to ask him what I was having. Pasta fazool."

"Thank you," I replied and looked at the menu to see if there was a description of the dish but, alas, could not find it listed.

When I looked up, I again heard the same voice.

"They spell it F-A-G-I-O-L-I, but for me its F-A-Z-O-O-L, the way it sounds."

"And it's good?"

"The best. It's one of the little things that have sustained me through my reasonably happy life. Some places make it different. Some places don't put in enough beans, and some overcook the pasta . . . but this place makes it just right, just the right combination of things done right. As with one's life, who can ask for more . . . but you? You enjoy your spaghetti and meatballs. It's why you came here."

"It is?"

"Sure," the old man replied. "I notice things like that. You don't last as long as I have unless you manage to keep your ears and eyes wide open."

He then gestured to me to approach.

"Here. Come share my table," he urged. "My business is done for the day and company is almost as much comfort as my bowl of pasta fazool."

I said thank you and joined him, just as the noisy and rude couple made their exit, arguing all the way.

"Such disrespect," the old man noted.

"To each other," I added.

"No," he disagreed, "to good food and to good digestion. Their stomachs will object soon enough, I assure you. By the way, you may call me Don Minestrone, resident wise man, *consigliore,* and former . . . well, never mind. It's all water under the bridge. Garlic that's already been pressed."

"What is?" I asked.

"The life I've lived. That's solely my affair. Now, the lessons I've learned, that's something I will share. Enjoy your pasta, and let me tell you a few stories, a word to the wise, guy."

. . . and so he did.

Herewith, some of the tasty morsels from our conversation . . . a few servings of

*P*asta *F*azool for the *W*iseguy's *S*oul

On the
Gentler Sex

——◆◆◆——

Maybe the guys running witness protection should consider a "relocation/divorce in absentia program." For some wiseguys this would be an offer they wouldn't want to refuse.

The Theory of Relativity

$\mathcal{D}$onny Benedetto had his own theory of relativity:

"Everything is relative," he used to say, then would add, "y'know, related."

He would then point to his nose and say, "See this nose; same as Tony Bennett's nose, and Bennett's name before he changed it was Tony Benedetto."

Donny was always looking for connections.

Like if a ref had anything to do with an unexpected point spread.

Or if a sudden flood of Cabbage Patch dolls had anything to do with a reported border seizure of unsafe toys from China.

Or if the only guy with a clean record who has served on three different crews might be a little too cozy with the boys in blue.

Donny had a good eye and he had a good mind.

He saw the connections before anyone else did.

Which is why everyone was surprised when Donny married the horse-faced bimbo he knocked up, particularly since he talked about dumping her the week before.

This was one connection that he didn't see.

. . . the fact that underboss "Horseface" Degrassi had the same last name as Donny's bimbo . . . not surprising since she was his niece.

And remember: shylocking a woman is different than shylocking a man.

Sure, you can command respect via the vig . . . but what does it get you?

Moreover, loans made to a woman have a way of turning into gifts and in no time at all the shylock is paying vig for favors that are way too fleeting.

Don't loan it, just call it a gift, and be clear that you expect something in return . . . something which you may or may not be able to kick a piece of upstairs later on.

The Love of a Good Woman

I wouldn't have made it through that stint upstate if it wasn't for the love of a good woman.

Gina was there—every weekend.

And I mean she was really there . . . there for me.

She didn't lambaste me with problems about getting by with me away, hassles from my friends and foes, or hassles from *her* life.

She was there for me, reminding me of the good times we had together. Saturday nights at the Copa, the weekends in Vegas . . . and the occasional quickie during a busy weekday afternoon.

And on the day of my release, she was there to pick me up and drive me back to the city.

. . . but first a stopover at a roadside motel where she proved that she hadn't let herself go to pot while her old man was in stir as we made up for some of the thirty-six months I was away.

It was almost worth the time I lost for the time I had.

Too bad I had to cut it short.

The parole board had sent out an advance notice of my release, and the wife was expecting me home for dinner.

Saving the Planet

*M*ama Mancini had convinced Don Mancini that "for the sake of the planet and our children's children" this thing of ours needed to get involved with recycling.

This, of course, created a few problems for the rank and file, whose job it was to destroy any and all evidence that might be used against us.

Betting slips, up in smoke (not recycled).

Handgun from a hit, in the river (not recycled).

Getaway cars, by necessity gas guzzlers (haven't seen a Prius yet that could outrun a five-year-old police cruiser).

Sure, we could crush boosted cars after they had been stripped . . . but we did that already and Mama knew it.

So that was when Ely the Enforcer (who was known to complain about his bad back after a night of shoveling and was always looking for everyone to chip in on the next order of lime) had a suggestion that all of the crew supported.

A week later Ely showed the don a deed to a business establishment that would provide numerous "recycling opportunities" for the family business.

And he showed it to Mama.

. . . who never brought the subject up again.

(By the way, the dog food factory was in the black within six months; that's what I call fiscally responsible recycling.)

Loved Ones

$\mathcal{T}$he Big Man Upstairs was a big advocate of family values . . . that's not to say that guys couldn't be guys with the whole nine yards—wife, mistress, girlfriend—you just made sure that you didn't bring shame or embarrassment to the home.

So when Shelly the Jew died in the saddle with his twenty-two-year-old mistress, Heather, the Big Man took measures to protect one of his favorite goddaughters, Shelly's wife of twenty-two years, Imogene, from undue suffering.

Shelly's lifeless bulk was redressed and taken out back of the social club where some of the guys had rigged up a weight set, thus making it look like the old guy had fatally strained himself in some feat of strength.

The word spread like wildfire and everyone flocked to Imogene's side to support her in her time of need, and extolled the virtues of her departed husband, a man dedicated to his chosen profession and to his family. (Indeed, the Big Man Upstairs stressed to all of his crew that they need to assert how loyal and true Shelly had been.)

When the Man Upstairs made his appearance at the wake, Imogene ran into his arms in thanks.

The Man Upstairs thought to himself that he had pulled it off . . . until she whispered in his ear, "I hope someone is being as supportive to Heather; she's a young thing and will probably miss him more than I will."

Gia

*M*rs. Enrica Campollini lived outside of Palermo.

A widow of independent means, she was also the proud mother of five beautiful young girls, virgins all, and all named Gia because in Italian, Gia means "Queen."

Though her husband was now long gone, a victim of mishap rather than malice, she nonetheless kept her contacts within the five families in the United States that he had had dealings with, and let it be known that she wished her daughters to become Americans.

So when it came time for mothers in the five families to seek out "good girls" for their sons to marry, Enrica made her Gias available and no one was dissatisfied.

Not the mother of the groom.

Not the mother of the bride.

. . . and definitely not the groom, as all of Enrica's daughters were as beautiful as their mother.

Soon Mama Campollini had all five daughters married to the scions of the five families in the United States, and in doing so had set herself up as the back-channel peacemaker for family disputes.

No personal problems were ever allowed to escalate to "business" problems without a consigliore's trip to Palermo so that Enrica could work her persuasion.

For Enrica means "leader of the house" and through her own keen matchmaking she had filled her house with all five families.

Carina

*C*aprice Capriani had five daughters and she named them all Carina.

The five daughters had five different fathers (as such things often happened when one's mother's name means "by whim") but all had indeed left their mother and her daughters well cared for . . . possibly unaware of the assistance provided by one another.

Caprice also paired her daughters off with the scions of the five families, though as American-born and Brooklyn-bred they required neither an entry to citizenship nor contract of marriage to ensure their protection.

As Enrica had done from Palermo, Caprice had done from Bensonhurst, and together the two sisters assured that there would be peace in the families, if not in their households.

. . . and to this day no one has ever complained.

Your wife doesn't need to know that you have a mistress.

And your mistress doesn't need to know that your wife is a better cook.

On Being Authentic

*Shakespeare once said,
"To thine own self be true."*

*He didn't mean spill your guts and
cut a deal (hear that, Henry Hill? hear that,
Sammy Gravano?) . . . he meant be "the real thing,"
not some poseur.*

*Wiseguys don't act like wiseguys;
they* are *wiseguys.*

Not Like in the Movies

I like movies as much as the next guy.

Love Scorsese, would watch anything he directed even if it was a piece of Japanese cartoon crap.

. . . but I never take them too seriously, and anyone who derives "life lessons" from them is a fool.

Too many of the kids today think they know the real thing since they saw it on the big screen.

Point One—You don't learn to shoot by watching a John Woo film or a gangsta video.

That holding-the-gun-sideways crap?

C'mon.

I'm not saying you need to aim every shot, but be real.

Point Two—In our line of work nobody needs a .44 Magnum.

It's unnecessary and it's impractical.

I can't tell you how many guys I know got a concussion from the recoil of one of those cannons as they tried to make like Eastwood with that phony hands-out-front stance.

(Boom! Next thing you know you're out cold when the recoil drives the gun up and straight back to make contact with your oh-so-soft noggin.)

Point Three—There is no driving music soundtrack to tip you off when the jig is almost up . . . and anybody who says "I never saw *it* coming" was just not paying attention.

I will give one point to the movies for honesty (and I think it was a Scorsese picture, because Marty gets this type of thing right): you can't get good spaghetti and marinara in the Witness Protection Program (and egg noodles and ketchup just isn't an acceptable substitute).

Headshrinkers

$\mathcal{D}$espite what you might have seen in the movies or on cable, real wiseguys don't have their heads shrunk.

Never.

They don't do it with funny nebbishy guys and they don't do it with tough high-class professional broads either.

Wiseguys don't talk about their inner feelings, and what goes on inside their heads is what they call proprietary information.

Jamie "Garbo" (short for Garbowski, because he preferred to work "alone," at least according to some of the older guys) thought he was depressed and contemplated having his head shrunk.

By the fifth session he was feeling a lot better—he had gotten fed up with the shrink's prying questions and finally punched him out.

As it turns out that's all he needed to get back on track.

Now "Garbo" punches out at least one guy a week and he's never been a better earner.

Madison Philly's wife talked him into going to see one of those Park Avenue shrinks to discuss their "bedroom problems."

The shrink was just out of college and seemed always distracted by money matters.

When Philly saw his wife with a moony gleam in her eye as she watched the shrink cross the room for a prescription pad he immediately knew what would save their marriage.

Philly agreed to pay double for her private sessions with Dr. Dreamy as long as she stopped talking about their "problems."

And just like that all of their "bedroom problems" went away, and most of Dr. Dreamy's financial ones as well.

The Borough of Kings

*W*hen wiseguys reminisce about the past, you hear them talking about the shows they saw at the Copa, the Lennox, the Apollo, and the Peppermint Lounge . . . but most of that is just big talk.

Why go to Manhattan when you can make the talent come to Queens or Brooklyn?

There used to be a great place out by Flatbush and Avenue U where any given weekend you could see the likes of Sinatra (okay, Sinatra Jr.) or Avalon or Rosselli.

There was another place out by JFK that also landed the headliners.

Strange thing, I think they both had "Airport" in their names . . . whatever.

And whereas in "the Big City" you might be treated with respect, in the borough of Brooklyn you would be treated like a king.

That's one of the reasons why it's always useful to patronize businesses closer to home.

(It is also worth noting that both of these places had easy and discreet access to bird sanctuaries and Jamaica Bay . . . just in case some other patron made the mistake of ruining your night out on the town in the borough of Queens or the county of Kings.)

The "Mafia" Exposé

*E*verybody was happy when Frankie Calzone finally got out of the slammer after a double-deuce run upstate.

Frankie had had a tough time of it.

His wife left him.

His mother moved back to Sicily, setting up housekeeping with his father's brother.

. . . and, to top matters off, his lawyer served him with papers the day he was released, hoping to recoup six figures of legal fees.

What was worse was that the lawyer already had a plan in place to squeeze blood from the stone that was Frankie's financial state . . . he wanted him to pull a "Valachi."

Joe Valachi was the first guy to open his mouth in print on this thing of ours.

Other guys had talked to the cops.

That goes without saying.

Valachi went one better . . . he talked to a writer and proceeded to throw the Gravano [ed. note: "the bull," as in Sammy "The Bull" Gravano] about all of our family business practices and alleged secret histories of our organization . . . which is to say he made it up out of whole cloth and passed it off as cold, hard facts, leaving the public no more informed than they were before.

That was close to sixty years ago . . . and the problem was that in the time that has passed, reality has mirrored a lot of those fictions and even Mario Puzo has helped to shape the evolution of our way of doing business. Some have even used the written word to settle old scores or distract the authorities in certain matters of guilt and innocence.

So, feeling quite desperate and having nowhere else to turn . . . he's still en route to freedom from the pen, after all . . . the thieving *goniff* of a lawyer was the guy to pick him up . . . Frankie signs the book contract and agrees to do lunch in a few days with a fat middle-aged bottle-blond broad (who used to change the spelling of her name every few months under the advice of her astrologer) who some simpleton appointed publisher.

Frankie's problem was simple.

He really didn't have any stories to tell.

Sure, he'd heard stuff . . . but that was other people's stuff.

And, of course, he didn't want to rat anyone out.

Hell, what was the sense of spending time in the can if you're going to spill your guts later on?

So what did Frankie do?

He turned back to the only guys he could trust . . . us.

All of the old gang got together in the back room of the Jamaica Bay Yacht Club that was built on the site of the old Little Cricket Steak House, which had spontaneously combusted a few years back . . . by the way, they never did identify that unfortunate fellow that was inside at the time . . . and put together some howlers.

It was virtual "can you top this" of mob lies.

Sally Mann suggested he tie us in to the Masons.

Joey the Loop brought in the Tri-Lateral Commission.

. . . and Old Man Carlucci called his aunt back in the old country, who provided Frankie with quite a list of names off tombstones in a neglected cemetery on the outskirts of Palermo.

We made up enough for a virtual library of mob stories, so, needless to say, Frankie was well prepared for his lunch with the publisher.

She was duly impressed and promised the book would get a big push and handed over the check . . . which the lawyer quickly claimed, wiping clean Frankie's debt to him.

As luck would have it, the book never got published.

Whoever hired that broad as publisher soon wised up and out she went.

The new publisher came in, looked at the now-completed manuscript, and had some reservations about it.

Not its veracity, mind you.

She was concerned that it lacked a . . . what did she call it . . . a female protagonist.

. . . but since the book had already been accepted, she just canceled the book and never asked for the advance monies back, adding it to the numerous unearned sums of her predecessor's "sure-thing" acquisitions.

So Frankie comes back to us and says, "Well, I got the rights back . . . why don't I try to sell it and we can all share in whatever it makes?"

We were touched.

Frankie remembered those who had helped him and now wanted to pay us back.

. . . but what about that female protagonist problem?

Frankie had the answer.

When the new publisher at a different house, who was of course the old publisher from the previous house (evidence of a long-standing tradition of every major house sharing in providing for the real losers in the industry), asked about the female protagonist, a concern that she herself had had earlier on but had kept to herself (at least in her version of the truth), Frankie answered, "That's because we're all gay." (And Frankie thought he saw dollar signs appear in her eyes . . . and thus, *Naked Came the Godfather* was signed to a seven-figure contract.)

The Inside Story

$\mathcal{J}$immy the Shank claimed to have been involved with some of the biggest heists in mob history.

You know, Lufthansa, Brinks, etc., and he used to love going to the movies (like *Goodfellas* and *Robbery*) and saying loud enough so that anyone sitting near him in the theater could hear it, things like "Nah, didn't happen that way," "Just another fairy tale" . . . and most of the time he would be right even if he really wasn't speaking from personal experience.

Wiseguys never spill the beans on the good stuff.

So when you see a movie where they claim to have had a "technical consultant"—most of the time it's some guy who is collecting a paycheck for lying.

Well, as we all recall, Jimmy the Shank went to his final reward right at about the same time his son Marty started film school.

Marty had idolized his dad and wanted to make him proud.

So once he got his degree, he came back to the neighborhood hoping to line up some "financing" for a movie he wanted to do.

Everybody had liked Jimmy and thought Marty was a good kid, so we were all willing to kick in a few Gs for the kid's project (who knows? He could be the next Spielberg or something), but Papa Gino, to whom all of us deferred, wanted to know a little something about the project first.

Marty told him that he wanted to do his own script and make the first "real-life-as-it-actually-is mob film."

Papa Gino was concerned, so he asked to see the script first, to which Marty quickly complied.

It was a good script . . . too good . . . the type of movie that would give away secrets that shouldn't be given away.

So Papa Gino called in Marty and said that he would fully back the movie . . . but only if he made a few changes first.

"Like what?" Marty inquired.

"Well, for one, it needs to be set in the world of Washington, D.C., K Street lobbying."

Marty realized without even being told that the first "real-life-as-it-actually-is mob film" was dead in the water . . . but he also realized that Papa Gino was willing to give him his shot at the big time, so he agreed.

He was about to accept the check from the generous old man when it dawned on him.

"What do I know about D.C. lobbying?" he admitted to his sponsor.

"Don't worry about it," Papa Gino replied. "I'll hire you some lobbyists as technical consultants and then you can shoot your script as is with just a few changes here and there."

After all, as everyone knows, lobbyists can lie better than wiseguys any day of the week.

Setting the Record Straight

Sometimes you just have to set the public straight, and that's what Joe Colombo did when he headed up the Italian-American Civil Rights League.

The group turned its attention to what it perceived as cultural slights against Italian-Americans, using boycott threats to force companies to withdraw commercials the league objected to, and also got to order the Justice Department to stop using the word "Mafia" in official documents and press releases, particularly interchangeably with "organized crime." The league also secured an agreement to omit the terms "Mafia" and "Cosa Nostra" from the film *The Godfather* and also succeeded in having Macy's stop selling a board game called *The Godfather Game*.

After all, some stereotypes are just downright demeaning and, back in the early seventies, grassroots organization to apply social and economic pressure was the right way to do things.

Nobody likes to be laughed at, and more than that, nobody likes someone else to make a buck off someone else laughing at you.

Though Joe is no longer with us (God rest his soul), there are still some around who are willing to take a torch (or more correctly, a burner) to the money-grubbing malefactors of cinematic humiliation of this thing of ours.

Sometimes things are just laughably bad. *Jane Austen's Mafia* comes to mind. (Be real—who's gonna believe Jay Mohr and Christina Applegate as Cosa Nostra?)

Fuhgeddaboudit.

. . . but sometimes you need to nip things in the bud so that you don't wind up with franchises of *Misc. Mafia Bad Guy Films #1, #2, #3*, etc.

In those cases, "Showbiz" Santoro has the easy course of action:

"Contrary to popular belief, it is not the critics that determine a successful franchise but rather the cash on the barrelhead, which is probably why there is no *Goodfellas Returns* but there are already three *Rush Hour* films.

"And now with the whole second market for DVDs and on-demand cable, the criminals who run Hollywood are always ready to squeeze every cent out of every picture they make.

"So when they make a picture I don't like, rather than speak my mind and thus give it more press, I quietly undercut it by helping reach a larger audience through nontraditional channels that add to my own bottom line . . . or in other words: I bootleg the sucker as fast as possible so no one ever has to pay full price to see the dog, so that no matter how popular it turns out to be, the studio hardly makes a dime.

"Nowadays, who needs a stagehands union slowdown when you can use a DVD burner to make your displeasure really felt while making your tidy profit as well."

Patron of the Arts

*C*razy Joe Gallo was a patron of the arts.

Now, I'm not talking about the fact that he was well read and liked opera and all that stuff.

I mean a real patron—someone who contributes in order to support and/or further advance the arts.

Word had gotten around that some guys were making a low-budget movie out of Jimmy Breslin's book *The Gang That Couldn't Shoot Straight,* which was loosely based on some of Joe's and his brothers' exploits.

Joey wasn't real pleased with some of the depictions in the book, so he reached out to the actor that had been cast in the role of Kid Sally (the Joey character) and suggested they have a sit-down. The actor was taken aback . . . but when Joey explained that he should bring a date and that they would double for the evening, some of the tension abated.

The actor—who by the way was Jerry Orbach, later on of *Law and Order* fame—met the gangster for a meal where Joey quickly explained that he wasn't trying to discourage him from playing the part. He just wanted him to get the part right and the only way he could do that was by getting to know him personally.

As any thespian knows, such an opportunity is truly invaluable for the craft of acting and the fact that Joey unselfishly gave of his time and self for the arts is truly inspiring.

Joey and Jerry became friends (there are even rumors that Jerry was present on the night of Joey's bloody demise at Umberto's Clam House).

(Also of note is that one of the minor performers in the film who doesn't play a mobster, just a con artist, is a guy named Robert De Niro who, like in his later role in *Godfather II*, winds up speaking most of his lines in Italian.)

Writing Well of the Dead

*W*hen it come right down to it, a man is remembered by his mug shot and his obit, and sometimes there is nothing you can do about the former, but Artie the Author was always willing to lend a hand on the latter.

Artie had a flair for words and a gift for spin usually not seen north of 1600 Pennsylvania Avenue.

And he always told the truth—well, at least sorta.

When Patsy the Panderer passed away, he came up with the line "affectionately remembered by his co-workers and subordinates."

When Harry the Hijacker went off the road, he called him "a teamster's teamster, if not in the union log books, at least in his heart."

And when the Scarpacci mob was gunned down after that little disagreement on the Super Bowl points spread, who can forget his expressions of "celestial camaraderie."

Only occasionally does this literary master have to stretch the truth a bit.

No one wants to read about a once-notorious gangland chieftain who died after a long illness and a prolonged stay in some Bronx nursing home (images of the drooling Capone immediately pervading everyone's consciousness).

No, indeed . . . and this is where some say Artie was at his best:

"After years of close supervision and constant surveillance, XXXX went to his eternal rest with his secrets intact. Those who knew the wizened mobster marveled at his discipline and discretion as many revealed (on a confidential basis, of course) the sagacity of the master, who freely offered counsel to those who deserved it while playing the fool for those whom he deemed beneath contempt."

Not just a nice turn of phrase, but a sort of "emperor's new clothes" kicker that served to hold the tongues of those who might wish to contradict this glorious memoriam.

Shylock and Showbiz

*T*he Silverman brothers managed to become something of a legend in these parts.

Shylock and Showbiz, as they were called, were from a long line of goniffs and decided that it was time for the family to diversify.

So Shylock took some of the cash on hand from the family coffers and put it out on the street for a lucrative return, while Showbiz started to dabble in the blue-movie biz while taking a financial position in a few clubs of various sorts.

What was soon evident was that the boys managed to fuel each other's bottom line.

Blue-movie stars were always looking for "a line" to finance their next "line" (that is, "a line of credit" to finance their next "line of coke"), and as a result Show would send them Shy's way, and Shy would do the same when a client needed to cover a vig with the endowment they might have left.

This sort of cooperative relationship was much more genteel than the earlier days of leg-breaking and white slavery . . . and everyone profited, each in their own way.

Soon Showbiz had his own top-flight club, boasting the best B-level acts the outer boroughs had to offer (including some singers who actually almost made the charts less than a decade ago).

And you wanna know something?

Stars who've been to the top and are now on the slide have the same sort of problematic financial planning situations that the blue-movie stars had in Showbiz's previous endeavor . . . and of course Brother Shy was always there to offer a line to make ends meet . . . a line whose vig might be cashed out by a return engagement at half the price of before.

Need I point out that more than a few acts found themselves regularly booked at bargain prices and the Brothers Silverman had found themselves a new family business?

Pacino

*N*o actor is more identified with this thing of ours than Al Pacino.

Talk about Michael Corleone personified.

But Frankie the Fan pointed out recently that he has probably played more cops and lawyers than mob guys (and before we go any further, that guy in *Dog Day Afternoon* may have been a criminal but he wasn't a mob guy, and the same goes for that junkie in *The Panic in Needle Park*).

. . . I mean, just look at some of his parts.

Serpico.

Heat.

Sea of Love.

Cruising.

. . . and then you throw in the three roles he did as lawyers . . .

And Justice for All.

City Hall.

The Devil's Advocate.

When you think about him and the mob—and I mean the real "mob," not the funny guys fighting Dick Tracy—it was pretty much Michael and Lefty and that's about it.

(And before anyone brings up De Niro, sure, he played Don Corleone in *GF#2* and the crazy don in those Billy Crystal films and the mook in *Mean Streets*, but his other mob parts cast him as either an Irishman or a Jew or an inbred mental defective in *Bloody Mama*—not exactly the sort of image that comes to mind when you say "godfather" . . . if you know what I mean.)

Hanging Out with the Wiseguys

*O*ver the years some things have loosened up.

The wall between this thing of ours and civilians sometimes becomes a little porous.

Back in the day it was Frank and Sam (that's Sinatra and Giancana . . . and if you had to ask, shame on you).

Then Joey and Jerry (Gallo and Orbach) . . . and so on.

Yeah, celebrities are different and not everyone has to worry about waking up with a horse's head in their bed, but nowadays even the social clubs are loaded with hangers-on and wannabes flashing more cash than they can afford and loaded down with enough bling that Dutch Schultz would never have to cast a set of concrete overshoes again.

They think they're in—they're connected— they're living the high life.

Just remember what Tommy Del said about hanging with Nicky Scarfo (at least according to George Anastasia):

"When you get involved with him, you know, you take the good and take the bad. . . . The good is you can run around a lot and have everybody in your circle afraid of you because you got Nicky behind you. The bad is, once in a while you get to do him a favor" . . . and, needless to say, you can't refuse (and that goes for the little lady hangers-on as well).

Confessions are a personal matter, never to be done in public nor in the presence of the police.

On Family

---

*You don't get to choose your relatives,
for better or worse.*

'Nuff said.

Weddings and Funerals

Sometimes it seems like the only time you can get the entire family together is for weddings and funerals. . . and sometimes the two are related.

(And I'm not just referring to the amount of times you've heard a distraught and disappointed father telling his daughter that the only way he is going to allow her to marry that #$@&*%!!! is over his dead body.)

Kid Sally the Suit summed it up this way:

Marriage is a beautiful thing.

It's a merger where both sides swap their stock equally in anticipation of future gains.

It's not just two people.

It's two families . . . well, except in the case of the Angelos, who always seem to marry their cousins, which might have something to do with their families' declining IQ, if you know what I mean.

It's filled with promise and the expectation of life.

Funerals, on the other hand, well, just reverse everything I said.

Somewhere along the way someone failed.

With natural causes . . . it's the individual's own constitution.

With less than natural causes . . . say, incidental projected-lead poisoning in doses of .22 and .38, it's usually the individual himself to blame.

. . . and did we fail him more than he failed us?

Either way, it's a sense of loss and the curtailment of a life.

And in both cases, there's always the rest of us, whether we be the best man, the undertaker, the flower girl, or the shooter.

We all have our part to play.

We all have to show up and watch everybody watching everybody else.

Who's happy, who's sad . . . and sometimes the answers to those two questions determine how soon there will be that next new life or indeed that next guest of honor at the affair that isn't the wedding.

And both require your best suit, of course . . . unless you are the guest of honor, at which point you rent or you don't care, since it's somebody else's problem now anyway.

Professionals

*M*ama Gino (who was harder and more business-savvy than Papa Gino on any day) always made the point that there is a difference between family and hired help.

Now, that's not to say that hired help is to be disrespected.

Far from it.

One must assume that the hired help is professional, or else why would someone bother paying them to do some job in the first place?

There are occasions where the simple, directed execution of a task by an uninvolved third party is the best way to do things.

Sometimes in these matters, family just gets in the way, because whether we like to admit it or not, every family has its own Fredo (Corleone, not Gonzalez, though the difference is minor).

Look at the comic book and movie about that hitman and his kid [ed. note: *The Road to Perdition* by Max Allan Collins]—everything was nice and professional until the big boss's son, played by the guy who played James Bond, screwed things up.

Or look at that Prizzi picture [ed. note: *Prizzi's Honor* by Richard Condon].

The professionals acted professional, but in the end the interests of the family won out.

Which brings up the flipside of the matter—just because they are family doesn't mean that they are going to act professionally.

That's not what they get paid for.

It would be nice if they're competent.

It would even be better if they are good . . . which is why education and training is so important.

This thing of ours is an unforgiving business.

We pay for the best . . . and expect to get what we pay for.

. . . and we expect the best from the family and are willing to pay so that they can provide it.

Senior Adviser

*E*ven after Don Carlo retired and passed management duties off to Little Carlo, the revered old man liked to keep his hand in the business, sort of like the consigliore that Don Corleone thought he was going to be to Michael until his grandson gassed him to death with DDT among the tomato rows.

(Don't tell me that kid wasn't trying to make his bones at an early age. Did you see that look of glee on his face as he got back at Grandpa for scaring him with the fruit peel in his mouth?)

But I digress . . .

So Don Carlo was often sought out for his advice.

Sometimes out of need.

Sometimes out of respect.

And sometimes just to make the old man happy.

Unfortunately, as these things sometimes go, eventually the old man began to lose it.

You know, his spaghetti plate was short a meatball or two.

So, anyway, it was soon widely agreed upon that the revered former don could no longer be trusted with the delicate information concerning our affairs.

As a result, fewer of the crew stopped by.

Most of the young guys didn't know him back in the day when he could give Giuliani a run for the money in business and broads . . . and Little Carlo had his hands full with special prosecutors, turncoats, and book deals.

So it fell to Baby Carlo to make sure that his grandfather was being looked after.

The first thing he did was hire a set of twin strippers who were working their way through nursing school as live-in aides for the old guy, and then he made sure that he scheduled lunch with him once or twice a week.

Unfortunately, as these things go, Don Carlo's condition continued to deteriorate, and more than that he became depressed and morose.

"I guess no one needs an old man's advice anymore," he'd say wistfully.

But then Baby Carlo got an idea.

One Wednesday afternoon he came in to the former don's room for their usual luncheon . . . but this time he had a present for the senior consigliore, an intercom.

"You know, Grandpa," Baby Carlo explained, "everybody misses your advice . . . but given the precariousness of your health, the doctors say we have to limit your visitors . . . too many germs, y'know."

"Such problems," the old man sighed.

"But you see, now with this intercom you can listen in on conversations with delicate matters . . . and then during our lunches you can feed me your advice, which I will bring back to the crew."

"We'll see," said the old man.

The following week Baby Carlo was amazed at the transformation in his grandfather, who was full of life . . . and advice.

"I didn't realize how long I've been away from day-to-day operations . . . and some of these new guys. . . . Whoever heard of names like Big Pussy and Ray Luca? . . . But the business never changes . . . and this is what you need to do . . . ."

And when Baby Carlo had gone through all of the Scorsese, *Sopranos,* and other mob stuff on

DVD . . . he just started over again in a different order and his grandfather was never the wiser.

The fact of the matter was one of his nurses never made it to graduation. Instead of her BS, she earned her MRS as Mrs. Don Carlo . . . that was a testimony to his turnaround of health.

He still wasn't hitting on all cylinders and he couldn't really be trusted in the driver's seat for very many things . . . but that didn't matter.

Life wasn't bothering him anymore.

He had a reason to live.

A new wife.

A grandson who listened to him.

. . . and of course Tony Soprano and the boys, who always seemed to need his advice, which he was more than willing to share.

Pets

*T*here are always going to be times when a wiseguy needs the type of friendship and uncomplicated affection that his compadres just can't provide (and of course his wife or *gumare* can't even fathom). These are the moments when the mobster in the know turns to a more complacent and furry companion . . . namely a pet.

When it comes to companionship, you just can't beat the animal kingdom, and the furry favorite of the fraternity is usually feline.

Indeed in that crucial first scene in *The Godfather*, what is in Don Corleone's lap? A cat, of course.

Oh, but that's just a novel written by a civilian.

True . . . but consider these other examples.

Joey Gallo, for instance.

Nobody is going to debate his status as a real mob guy.

And what type of a pet did he have?

A cat.

A very large one, in fact, one from Africa with a full and flowing mane of hair. It proved to be quite useful in encouraging deadbeats to pay up on their debts.

Lefty Ruggerio, of *Donnie Brasco* fame, also kept an African kitty cat as a pet. It had a voracious appetite and (if that cop Pistone is to be believed) ate between twenty and thirty steaks a day. Not even a top-earning captain like Lefty could afford those type of butcher bills, so eventually the two had to part ways very reluctantly.

The cat never turned on Lefty . . . which is more than you could say about his supposed friend Donnie Brasco, who turned out to be a cop.

Mrs. Mandelina's Son

I kinda always felt sorry for Mrs. Mandelina, having to raise a son without a husband and all since Fat Frank got struck with that terminal indigestion over at Carlucci's at that dinner after he had had that conversation downtown with the DA.

Everybody agreed that it would be hands-off and the sins of the father would never be held against the son.

As to Little Frank's future . . . that was up to Mrs. Mandelina.

So when everybody saw how shy the little guy was and how timid and all, we just figured that the Mandelina line of enforcers was coming to an end.

After all, none of us really believed that a woman could raise a *mensch* . . . and if the kid was shy and timid, how would he ever get that oh-so-important education from the streets that has molded numerous generations of productive earners such as ourselves? And given the fact that we didn't want to interfere and all, we kinda sorta just left them alone.

A few months passed, fall, winter, spring, the usual . . . and lo to my wondering eyes appear Little Frank out there stealing hubcaps with the best of them.

As he raced past me I grabbed him by the collar and pulled him back so that I could extemporize some wisdom upon him.

"What's up?" I said. "You don't normally do this sort of thing."

"I do now."

"Why?"

"It's how my father got started."

"Who told you that?"

"My Uncle Phil."

"Oh yeah, what's he do?"

"Don't know . . . but he sure is tough."

"Where's he from?"

"Philadelphia."

(I shoulda known.)

I put his feet back in contact with the ground and let him rejoin the hooligans he was running with.

Who the hell was this guy Phil?

I needed to know, so I discreetly sauntered over to the Mandelina abode.

Not meanin' to pry, I discreetly asked how things were going with Little Frank.

"He's comin' out of his shell," she replied, ". . . and he's gonna be a better man than his father ever was, you'll see."

I asked who his father figure was, perhaps a new man in her life.

She laughed.

"Hardly . . . just my brother Phil."

I became serious and said, "Who's he connected with?" letting her know the slippery slope of letting outsiders operate within our territory.

"William Morris," she replied.

"Who's he?"

"Not he, them . . . it's an agency. He's an actor. I saw that my boy was getting a little soft, so I asked my brother the De Niro wannabe to talk to him and straighten him out. After all, one actor in the family is enough, if you know what I mean."

Indeed I did.

Chums

*U*ncle Frankie always thought weekend outings were a good idea.

I can remember many a Saturday or a summer Monday when he used to take my brothers and me out for some fishing out past Amboy's Light off the Rockaways.

He'd lend us some poles and we'd try our luck on whatever was running.

Uncle Frankie always had some of his guys as mates, usually Stevie the Weasel and Bendover Sal. Sometimes one of his partners, a guy named Charlie the Tuna or sometimes Charlie the Chum, used to come along, but he wasn't a serious fisherman. He just sat around drinking beer and telling stories.

I remember one summer Saturday, Uncle Frankie took us way out farther than we ever went before. My kid brother had been on my uncle ever since the two of them saw in *Jaws* that they had to go out real far and "chum" the water if we wanted to catch the big ones.

Uncle Frankie promised him we would, and sure enough, there we were way out to sea on that next Saturday.

My brother asked, "Did you remember to bring the chum?"

"Sure did," he replied, "and plenty of it, but you leave that to Stevie and Sal . . . after all, you need to concentrate on catching the big ones just like we planned."

I noticed Charlie wasn't around and asked Uncle Frankie about it.

"He won't be coming with us in the future. He's got too big a mouth . . . might scare away the fishes."

No sooner did we get out there than Stevie and Sal started chumming off one end of the boat while my brother, my uncle, and I fished off the other end.

Somewhere about late afternoon, the two chummers came to our side and said, "It's done."

My uncle announced it was time to head back to shore.

When my brother protested that he hadn't caught anything yet, I heard Sal remark that maybe Charlie had scared them all away.

Uncle Frankie had a quick solution, and baited my brother's hook one more time and had him drop the line right where the chummers had been working. He made sure that the hook had the biggest and bloodiest worm that was still left in the bait box, and before he tossed it over the side he whispered instructions to my brother to say, "Tell them Charlie sent you," which he did.

Sure enough, he got a bite almost immediately, a big one too, and we all headed back to shore.

We never did see that old chum Charlie again . . . I guess his big mouth must have exempted him from future trips.

Getting Out of Town

*U*ncle Frankie always encouraged us to get out of the neighborhood, get away from it all, and take a nice vacation free from the day-to-day hassles and gives-and-takes of this thing of ours.

Now, most, when they think of vacation, they think of Vegas or Atlantic City or even, at least in the good old days, Florida, but Uncle Frankie always advised against that.

He always advocated places like Jerome, Arizona, Manhattan, Kansas, and Renton, Washington (just to name a few). Nice quiet places where your business concerns won't get involved with their business concerns.

And besides that, there are good people all over and plenty of opportunities to stop and smell the roses.

And if, perchance, you come across someone you recognize who might have disappeared or entered the Witness Protection Program (since the Feds seem to prefer these out-of-mainstream locales), so much the better.

Just make a note of it or phone it in.

Someone else can take care of it.

No reason to spoil your vacation.

Vendettas

*V*endettas just don't make sense anymore unless you're sure that you're dealing with an only child of an only child.

In the old days sometimes you might have to wipe out a small village, but then you'd be done with it and be able to move on.

Ever since Vatican II, family ties have gotten fuzzier.

You don't just have to deal with a wife and mistress and their offspring, but you also sometimes need to keep in mind that there might be an ex-wife or two who also had some of his kids, not to mention larger-scale blended families and yadda yadda yadda.

I remember one godson who wound up being an uncle through marriage to his very own godmother.

No one wants to waste time having to do entire genealogical charts and family trees before getting the go-ahead for a hit, either larger or smaller.

It's just not efficient anymore, and efficiency is what it's about.

. . . and in the words of Hugo the Iceman, "Why can't we all just recognize the fact that we are all brothers? It didn't get in Cain's way, pure and simple."

———◆◆◆———

Honor your father and your mother . . . and make good on their bets when they can't. Medicare doesn't cover kneecapping.

———◆◆◆———

On Christian Charity

---

*No matter what you hear from any college boy,
God is an Italian.*

*. . . And those of us who have moved our
way up through the ranks take the moniker
of "godfather" very seriously.*

A Great Responsibility

*B*eing a man of respect is a great responsibility.

More than a doer and adviser, you also have to be an inspirer . . . you know . . . the type of guy that other people feel they should be like.

It's not just the money and the fear . . . it's the sense of obligation to make things better . . . to make things right . . . to ensure that true justice will prevail.

I remember that wonderful scene in Puzo's *The Godfather* during the early years of the don's rise to power.

Corleone's wife asked him for a favor (the type of request any married man with half a brain functioning knows that he can't refuse)—she wanted him to intercede with a tenement landlord on behalf of a woman and her son and his pet dog who were going to be evicted and thrown out into the street.

Now, if life was the way tabloids like the *New York Post* depicted it, Corleone would have threatened the man by having a few of his thugs stop by and maybe getting a little physical in their manner of persuasion.

Makes for nice headlines . . . but not the way things really work.

Corleone merely explained to the landlord, a Mr. Roberto, what the situation really was and provided him with a bit of Christian insight into the necessity of charity in this world of ours.

Mr. Roberto was touched (without being physically touched, I might add) and replied in a penitent and remorseful fashion befitting the sinner who wishes to forsake his fallen ways:

"Your good heart in helping this poor widow has shamed me and I wish to show that I, too, have some Christian charity. Her rent will remain what it was."

One man's, Corleone's, Christian act of charity inspires another to overcome his indulgence in greed for the sake of Christian charity.

One man leading by example, not by fear or threats. . . . And isn't that the way God wanted it to be . . . least of my brother do unto to me and all that stuff?

Lending God
a Helping Hand

*N*ever steal from the poor box, and always respect the church.

God is watching and will take care of his own.

So when the sacristy at St. Anselm's was robbed, lending a hand to ensure the culprits served the proper penance was not out of the question.

Another time, Monsignor Clancy was troubled about the "allegations" concerning his newest curate, who had been transferred five times in the last three years. He asked if someone could intercede if he steps "out of line" and did anything funny.

I pointed out that I respected the church.

He smiled and said fine. "God is watching and will take care of his own . . . if He's not there doin' the protectin' then go right ahead . . . out of respect for the church, of course."

Honor Among Thieves

*I*s it really too much to ask that there be honor among thieves?

After all, it's not like we are running for office or something.

Sure, everyone occasionally strays and succumbs to temptation, but once the error of one's ways has been pointed out, it is downright foolhardy to cut corners, particularly when the guy doing the pointing out is a good Catholic boy like Joe Colombo.

When a jewel-studded crown was stolen at Christmastime from a certain Brooklyn church, Joe Colombo, the good Catholic boy that he was, made some discreet inquiries and sent out the strong suggestion that whoever absconded with this most holy of relics during this most holy of seasons might want to consider reconsidering their actions and making proper restitution to the church for its missing crown.

No questions asked.

Now, Joe had become boss of the Profaci family (one of the original five families, I might note) after Joseph Magliocco had died of the usual "mysterious illness," and as such was the type of guy who was used to having his suggestions acted upon with undue haste.

As the thief was not a complete ignoramus, he quickly complied and arranged for the discreet return of the crown.

The only problem was that he kinda sorta got a souvenir for himself, a little token of compensation for time spent on the job so that things wouldn't be a total loss.

After all, who was going to notice three missing diamonds, given how gem-encrusted the crown was?

The answer to that question was, of course, Joe Colombo, who quickly felt compelled to rectify the situation and encourage the recalcitrant sinner to do penance.

Sure enough, the missing diamonds turned up, as did the body of the thief with a penitential rosary wrapped around his neck.

The Bishop's Legacy

*A*ngelo "The Bishop" Gianni retired from active duty twenty years ago when a stray bullet paralyzed him from the waist down. This, of course, didn't deter the Feds from trying to put him away for the rest of his years . . . but in the race with the Reaper, they lost out.

It was a close finish, though, as the IRS was on the verge of papering him with enough penalties to wipe out all of his savings, his home, and his other holdings, as well as incarcerating him for what would truly be a life sentence.

Now, Angelo's sister and all of her nun buddies took care of the old man and, on more than one occasion, he let us know that he wanted them taken care of (in the good way) after he had slipped this mortal coil.

Now, lucky for Angelo he passed away at the beginning of a four-day weekend, because this delayed the Feds from actually seizing his assets until after the funeral.

Unfortunately for the government coffers, everything Angelo owned was in his house, which suffered an unfortunate conflagration while everyone was at the funeral . . . a lovely affair even though more than a few of us were a bit tired from some heavy transport work that we had accomplished the night before.

By the time the Feds got there, there was nothing but a pile of ashes to sift through.

Everyone was shocked but heartened by the almost instantaneous release in the press that the beneficiary of the insurance policy on the place was not Angelo but the order his sister belonged to. This windfall allowed them to renovate their convent and community center, which now had a marvelous new entertainment center, DVD collection, and Jacuzzi—all inscribed with "AG."

The Bishop would have wanted it that way.

Christmas Shopping

$\mathcal{I}$ know some guys who just hate the hustle and bustle of the holiday season, and it's always nice when one guy lends a hand to another to make things a little easier.

Take John Jr., the Dapper Don's son.

According to the *New York Times*:

"John Jr., his wife, Kim, and several friends went on a late-night shopping spree at the Toys 'R' Us store in Douglaston, Queens. . . . Mr. Gotti's lawyer, Richard A. Rehbock, said the Gottis and six other couples—'Not associates,' he said, 'they're called friends'—got to the store at around 10:30 p.m. As many other stores have done, Toys 'R' Us extended its hours for the holiday season; this month it does not close until midnight. For almost two hours, the Gottis and their friends strolled aisles jammed with toys. Mr. Rehbock said that the Gottis and their friends were still inside when the store closed but that they and other remaining customers were allowed to finish their shopping—which store officials said is standard practice. He said that the group spent about $8,000 and that the Gottis planned to donate some of the toys to a children's home.

"'As I understand it, they bought toys for their various children,' Mr. Rehbock said. 'These children are not associates. They are children.'"

Now, what could possibly be wrong with this little piece of holiday cooperation and charity?

The answer is obviously *nothing*.

Now, if John Jr. had used his "celebrity" to grease the skids a little and perhaps arrange some private shopping for a few close friends, that would have been fine too . . . but he didn't, because, as the papers mentioned, during the holiday season such late-night shopping sprees were considered "standard practice."

In essence, it was one family man helping out a few other families, and that's all.

Of course the boys at the tabloids had to find fault and some circulated the rumor that John Jr. had also secured a full carton/crate of Tickle Me Elmos (the hard-to-get toy of that year) . . . but such allegations seem to have been fabricated.

And I am sure that if John Jr. had wanted a Tickle Me Elmo, there would have been one under his tree compliments of Santa.

A Shepherd and
His Flock

*T*here used to be a time when every neighborhood had their own little San Gennaro festival . . . now street festivals are a dying breed.

Carlo the Caboose (called such because of his none-too-dainty derriere) always did what he could to keep his local parishes interested in maintaining and/or continuing their yearly charitable street fairs.

Lord knows, the parishes need the money, what with the diocese always threatening to close them down for lack of attendance and such. (Yo, bishops, remember many of us still believe even when we don't make a presence every Sunday—and when was the last time you guys were doing unto the least of your brothers?) So Carlo always made sure that the ride guys and the food guys and the game guys were always being reasonable in their dealings with the pastors.

No problems needed to arise since there was always enough to go around for everyone.

I remember when St. Nico's parish took a turn for the worse and the parish elders (heck, the entire attending parish were now elders) were afraid that some of the young gangs and bangers were going to show up and cause trouble.

Carlo dispatched a few of his strong-arms to make sure that didn't happen.

A shepherd always has to watch out for his flock.

A smart wolf has to watch out for the other wolves as well.

———◆———

Remember—only confess to the Lord your own sins.
    (He already knows everybody else's, and he's
not going to squeal.)

———◆———

On Good Deeds
and
Acts of Kindness

---

*Always remember to do unto others,
because sometimes it's not your accountant
who is watching the balance sheet.*

Mrs. Santini's Trip to the Old Country

*M*r. and Mrs. Santini were fixtures of the old neighborhood.

They never had kids of their own but rather preferred to adopt all of the kids of the neighborhood.

They'd look out for them, and look after them in their parents' absence.

Hiding out from the bullies? Drop by the Santinis'.

Hiding out from your parents? Drop by the Santinis'.

Hiding out from the cops . . . well, you get the idea.

The Santinis never asked any questions and as long as you behaved and showed them the type of respect anyone should expect from a family member, you had a sanctuary.

. . . and this sanctuary continued well into our adult years.

It's not that they were oblivious to what was going on around them. Indeed, Mrs. Santini used to hold court on her stoop every morning with all of the other old neighborhood biddies, trading gossip and bragging rights to whatever was the news of the neighborhood.

They also had rules—don't come by for dinner unless you are bringing dessert, no funny boy-girl stuff if you're spending the night unless you got a license, and, of course, all personal firearms had to be disposed of before entering the premises.

. . . and, of course, you had to spend time with the Santinis if you were staying there; no eating and running, and of course you were expected to pay a modicum of attention to their tale-telling, whether it was about what was happening on the block or life in the old country (Sicily), where things were so much simpler. The two would lapse into their own little world and muse on the trip to Sicily they planned to make in the near future.

As these things usually go, Mr. Santini surrendered his mortal coil in advance of his Mrs., without either of them setting foot back in Sicily.

Mrs. Santini grieved a bit . . . but continued to do her duty as news keeper of the neighborhood and custodian of her own little safe house.

After a few months had gone by, a group of the boys got together to try to find out if they had any other family here or in the old country . . . but as it turned out their little world of two was indeed just a little world of two.

No relatives here.

No relatives there.

Mrs. Santini was all alone except for the neighborhood and, given her failing health and eyesight, would probably never cast her eyes on the beauties of Palermo ever again.

She pined for the old country but the trip would be too long and too involved (who knew if she had a passport or her citizen papers and in this anti-immigrant phase of our nation, no one wanted to open that can of soup) . . . but she could dream, and that would have to suffice . . . that is, until me and the boys came up with an idea.

We told her to pack a bag.

We had arranged a trip home to Palermo for her.

Just a short trip . . . but a trip nonetheless.

She became flustered.

What about my papers, the money, what if I get airsick?

No problem, we assured her, and lined up a limousine to take her out to Republic Field on Long Island.

We put her on a private plane with a trained nurse and a trained escort who were in on the deal, gave her some airsick meds to put her to sleep, and flew her down to a secluded condo in Boca Raton where a few of the old boys from the old country had gone to retire.

She was wined, dined, and reclined . . . all along thinking she was back in the old country.

A week later the route and process was reversed and she was back in her home with stories to tell.

Everything went off without a hitch.

That is, until two weeks later, when a guy from Homeland Security barged into my office and wanted to know who I had bought off at the TSA and passport control.

I was confused.

What was he talking about?

Then he told me.

It seems his nana lived down the street from Mrs. Santini, and when his nana complained about having to remove her shoes before being allowed to fly to Cleveland for a family funeral, Mrs. Santini was more than willing to offer her some advice.

"Why don't you ask that nice mobster who comes to visit me each week? He arranged my trip to Sicily and back, and I never had to go through security or anything. He's connected, you know."

Mrs. Mangione's Phone Bill

*M*rs. Mangione was like the nana I never had.

She was the grandmother of my best friend, Tony Z., who she raised since his own mom ran out on him and his dad was in the can.

She used to make the best cookies and she always made sure that Tony Z. got extra so he could share them with me. She even babysat me (though we looked at it as more of a sleepover vacation with Tony Z.) during that time my dad was doing upstate and my mom was otherwise engaged on his hardship appeal.

So when I found out that she was having some trouble making ends meet—Tony Z. having disappeared—I always made it a point of stopping by and making sure that she was wanting for nothing.

I remember that at one point I was a bit distracted. Rumor had it that the Feds had a new rat that they were in negotiations with . . . and as a result I missed my weekly appointment with Mrs. M.

Next week I dropped by and she was upset.

The cable company was switching Turner Classic Movies to the premium package, which was way out of her budget.

I looked over her bill and realized that I could get her a better deal that would combine her cable and phone service at a fraction of the price.

She agreed, anything to get back her beloved TCM.

Unbeknownst to her, I arranged to have her bills sent directly to me . . . no reason that she had to worry about such things.

Being a conscientious sort, I looked over her latest phone bill for ways to economize.

One way was to eliminate the number of collect calls she got from New Mexico—once a week, without fail.

Funny thing, Mrs. M. didn't know anyone in New Mexico . . . and the only ones who ever called her were family.

I didn't pursue the matter, not wanting to upset her.

I did, however, curtail those collect calls from New Mexico . . . and eliminated a rat problem as well.

A Rotten Kid

*W*hy is it that sometimes the nicest people have really rotten kids?

Take the Mallazos, who ran the Pizza Palace downtown.

Nicest people in the world.

Both of them.

Worked seven days a week.

Hired neighborhood kids for part-time work.

Didn't charge for deliveries.

Never caused anybody any trouble.

So how they wound up with a loser like their boy Mickey is beyond me.

Mickey was just a bad seed . . . always in trouble . . . dropped out of school . . . the whole nine yards. The only thing this bad kid never did was run away from home, making his parents' lives a living hell in their two-bedroom apartment above the pizzeria.

One night, in a fit of pique, he trashed the entire pizzeria and ran off with the week's receipts.

Well, at least that's what he tried.

You see, everybody at the social club had a warm spot in their hearts for the Mallazos and not just because they delivered up until midnight.

So a group of us got together and intervened.

The first thing we did was take Mr. and Mrs. M. out to look for their evil spawn . . . and while we were doing that we had the pizzeria torched—nice professional job with no damage upstairs so that the insurance company could help them rebuild the business their son tried to destroy.

We also found Mickey and got back the receipts (which, for the record, had been reported burned in the fire . . . the M.'s deserved a little bonus equity for all their hard work).

We also had Mickey write out a note to his parents telling them he was never going to darken their doorway again . . . and we then arranged him a nice and secure job with a firm named Halliburton (with whom we and several others have had deals in the past) that lined him up a job in the food-service business.

He made us promise that he wouldn't be sent anywhere too hot . . . and we agreed.

Who knew they also serviced bases in the Arctic Circle?

The Lemon, the Prize, and the Wreck

 S ometimes you have to encourage those who look up to you to do the right thing (and then you need to pull a few strings to make sure that they do).

Such is the case in a little story I like to call "The Lemon, the Prize, and the Wreck."

Dino the Dealer had gotten rooked.

The price that everyone said was too good for a low-mileage Lincoln was too good. The middleman had guaranteed that it had spent the last six months in a garage, undriven and off the street.

Turns out he wasn't lying . . . he just left out the fact that the garage was in New Orleans and underwater for the six months specified.

Dino needed to move it fast because he needed its space on the lot for the new model that was just coming in, the one he planned on driving around as a demo model, but his spiffy new chariot couldn't come in until the Louisiana lemon was moved out.

So Dino donated the lemon to the local church for a raffle, telling them as much about the car as he had been told originally, of course omitting its extended aquatic period.

(Needless to say, he wrote off the donation at its high and dry blue-book value as well.)

The church has the raffle, and the car is won by a single mother of three who is having trouble making ends meet.

In no time at all, the mom is having recurrent car trouble and can't afford to repair it, let alone pay the taxes the government wants on her winning of a luxury item.

She's frantic.

She doesn't know what to do.

So she does what any good neighbor lady should do in that position.

She goes to see her don and ask for advice.

The solution is simple, he tells her, wreck it and collect the insurance.

The only problem, she informs him, is that there is no insurance yet. The church had insured all of the prizes as a whole but none of that was transferable to the winners.

What about the previous owner? he asked.

She hesitated for a moment, then admitted that he claimed it was not his problem.

. . . and his name was?

The don nodded: he was "familiar" with Dino (and also familiar with Dino's submersible situation) and he assured her the situation would be taken care of forthwith.

Not long thereafter, Dino's new demo disappeared off the lot.

It had apparently been stolen and dumped by a junkyard where it was vandalized and crushed in the compactor.

Dino was mad. The insurance company had already given him a check but he knew it was going to play havoc with the negotiation of the renewal of his policy, so he went to the don for help and to request that he might intercede when the time for renewal came up.

The don asked him to bring the check, and because he was the don, Dino did.

The don told him to sign it, and because he was the don, Dino did.

The don then took the check from Dino and handed it to the mom.

Why? Dino cried.

Because it was not your car that went into the compactor . . . it was hers.

Then where is mine?

Safely parked, the don answered, tossing him the keys.

Where?

At the bottom of Dead Horse Bay, a stone's throw from the Belt Parkway.

Second Chance

*S*ometimes it takes a crucible for a guy to change his way of life.

Take Jimmy Fallone (or, as he was known in the hood, "Jimmy the Felon"). He was one of those guys who lived life to its fullest.

Cannoli for breakfast.

Lasagna or Parm for lunch.

Seven courses of somethings for dinner.

No exercise.

Lotsa scotch and disreputable companions (like me).

To all outward appearances, he was in perfect health and was widely considered to be at the top of his trade in problem disposal (he was known in the craft for his signature move of leaving a book of matches on the corpse with one match burnt out) until one lunch where he grabbed his chest and— boom bada bing—three hours later he was on the table getting a quadruple bypass, then a new kidney, and then an excision of the gallbladder followed by several stern instructions from numerous Middle Eastern doctors who advised him to change his lifestyle or invest in mausoleum realties.

And he did.

He ate healthier.

Exercised.

Saw his doctor regularly.

And encouraged his friends to do the same.

He also changed his calling card from a matchbook to an organ-donor card (complete with the victim's falsified signature, of course).

When asked about it, he shrugged and replied, "Waste not, want not."

A Sunday in Kenosha

*G*enie the Judge was strictly into stealing cars and flipping them to out-of-state or out-of-the-country secondhand dealers. For him, boosting a car for parts was a waste of time . . . though he was well acquainted with several associates who specialized in stripping whatever they could get their hands on for parts.

One such associate of his by the name of Chi Danello based his business out of Chicago. The usual plan was to boost the car in the city, take it to the suburbs for a strip, and then dump whatever was left somewhere off Highway 50 in Kenosha County, Wisconsin.

Genie was puzzled.

"Why go all the way out of state to dump the wrecks?"

Chi explained:

"One Sunday night I was coming back from a Packers game in Milwaukee, back when they used to play a few games there each season, when I started to have car trouble right outside of Kenosha.

"A few miles later, the car gave up, nada.

"Now, it was really rather late, and the weather was typical Wisconsin winter weather, and the roads were fairly deserted, so I figured that I was going to have to leave the car and trudge on down the road till I came to a place where I could call the AAA (this was back before cell phones and all).

"Much to my surprise, a kid pulled over in his pickup and offered me a ride. Turned out his father had a towing business and in no time at all we had reached his home.

"I told his father where the car was and we were back out the door to tow the car to the shop before the ravages of Wisconsin road salt caused permanent damage to my car.

"Father and son looked it over and gave it a fix while their Mrs. gave me some stew to take the chill out.

"Whatever it was, they got it fixed and sent me on my way with nary a bill for the service because it was Sunday and they didn't work on Sunday.

"So as a result, anytime I can provide them with the possible chance of some towing fees, I do . . . and I always make sure that it isn't Sunday, either."

Those Who Wait

*S*ome English guy named Milty once said something along the lines of "They also serve who stand and wait," and such was the case of Alfonse the waiter.

"The waiter" wasn't some kind of moniker, it was what he did . . . at Passante's in Bensonhurst. Alfonse wasn't a wiseguy, he was a civilian, but the type of civilian you could trust to only listen when you wanted him to and to only pay attention when he needed to.

He was always ready to take your order when the time was right and to present the check when the business was finished, whether everyone knew it or not.

He never screwed up an order or kept you waiting and never engaged in any annoying banter.

He was the perfect waiter and he'd been working at Passante's for close to fifty years.

Then one day, lo and behold, he didn't show up for work . . . and we all knew something was wrong.

Sure enough, Alfonse was sick, real sick, and he hadn't told anyone about it, and he had started cutting corners on his medications and wound up having a bad reaction.

It was then that we found out about Alfonse's private life—he had none, no family, no friends, nada . . . and now thanks to a prescription drug plan that only saved money for the insurance companies and the drug companies, he was almost penniless and way too sick to continue working.

We all liked Alfonse and though he wasn't "a friend of ours," we offered to chip in to help him make ends meet.

He refused—he wouldn't accept charity.

Now, as it turns out, unbeknownst to most, Big Ragu owned a piece of Passante's and Ron Zeroni (Big Ragu's father) was becoming a problem. The Feds were putting a case together that would put him away for twenty to thirty with good behavior, and the old guy's mind was failing, causing him to have a chronic case of running off at the mouth about things that needed to be left unsaid.

So Big Ragu called in Alfonse and asked him for a favor. Given his current situation, would he consider "confessing to the charges that were going to be pinned on the old man" and, in return, he would be guaranteed top-level medical care and the respect guaranteed a true "man of respect" in the can.

Alfonse paused for a moment and asked if it would really help the situation with his father, who had always been a perfect customer and a great tipper.

Big Ragu assured him that it would.

Alfonse nodded and soon found himself on the way to a lovely white-collar correctional facility with A-1 medical care.

Big Ragu also did a little preliminary spin on who Alfonse was, and some of the older inmates immediately treated him like, if not a don of dons, at least a capo of capos.

Moreover, someone from our crew would visit him every other week to make sure his needs were being met . . . and they were.

Alfonse was more than content, as he never dreamed that he would have the security to retire during his golden years and now all of his needs were being met by no less than the federal government itself.

Goodwill

Charity sometimes works hand in hand with common sense . . . and it should.

You should never pass up the opportunity to do a good deed, because, after all, charity is its own reward.

Say, for example, you have a certain amount of persuading that needs to be done on a recalcitrant client and, before you know it, your nice imported suit winds up with some unsightly stains on it.

Now, it's a well-known fact that stains sometimes contain DNA and as a result are very hard to remove from those sorts of fabrics used by the better suit-makers whose work we usually support.

So what do you do?

Suits can always be replaced.

So bite the bullet, so to speak, and get yourself another one.

. . . and what about the old one?

Get a quickie cleaning from a discreet establishment and donate it to Goodwill or perhaps one of those centers that loan out suits for interviews.

Charity is indeed its own reward . . . and sometimes it manages to obscure evidence as well.

Honest Cops

*H*onest cops.

You have to respect them.

They're just doing their job.

That's what my godfather always told me.

Now, that said, speaking from experience, the group in question is quite small, and to the best of my recollection a dying breed, so when Gino (my godfather) talks about such things, I usually just nod my head.

Now, Gino was getting on in years and was on his last legs with a bad ticker and a prostate problem to boot.

He knew he was on his way out.

So I'm stopping by one of his favorite eateries for some of their first-class minestrone to go when this cop taps me on the shoulder and says, "How's Gino?"

I give him the hairy eyeball.

He shakes his head and repeats the question. "How's Gino? I understand he's in a bad way."

"What's it to you?" I asked, throwing down a sawbuck for the soup, which had just arrived.

"Just tell him Sergeant Daniels sends his best."

So I deliver the soup and am about to leave when Gino asks if I ran into anybody. I say no but then remember the cop.

"Yeah, a Sergeant Daniels said he sends his best."

"That's nice," Gino said with a smile. "I always liked Daniels. He couldn't be bought, just wanted to keep the peace in the neighborhood. That's why he never moved up. I bet he's a few months shy of retirement."

A smile crossed Gino's face. He grabbed a piece of paper, wrote down a few words, asked for an envelope, and addressed it.

"When I go, drop this in the mail," Gino instructed. "Don't open it. It's none of your business. Do this for your godfather."

Gino passed the next week and I did as instructed. I didn't have to look at the address on the envelope to know that it was bound for Sergeant Daniels.

A few weeks later I read in the papers that Daniels had been promoted and was retiring a lieutenant, having closed three major cases of the past ten years in as many weeks, recovering close to $3 million in missing cash, bonds, and jewelry . . . all long written off and probably paid out by some insurance company.

Had Gino given me that tip, I would have had enough to retire in style.

But Gino knew Daniels was an honest cop, and he deserved this little something extra for a promotion before retirement.

Friends don't let friends get in over their head . . .
unless there is a real nice profit to be made and
you're assured of a substantial piece of it.

On Community Values

Politicians talk about the problems of NIMBY (not in my backyard) when they talk about undesirable projects like prisons and power plants. I say if you can't be trusted to look out for your community, how can you be trusted to protect anything?

The Changing Face of the Neighborhood

*B*ack when our family business first got its start here in the land of opportunity, we provided a service for the local businesses that the *pezzonovantes* wouldn't.

The politicians and the bankers and the police didn't care about the neighborhood.

We did.

And the neighborhood was grateful.

Well, Mario the Squid realized that it was once again time to turn our attentions to neighborhood concerns.

Corner delis were being replaced by grocery megastores.

Coffee shops were being driven out of business by hoity-toity designer coffee stores. (Five bucks for a stinkin' cup of coffee—forget about shylocking and making book, that's what I call an offense worthy of felony status.)

Little neighborhood restaurants were being shuttered by the likes of Olive Garden and Pasta House.

Not only are these artificial and plastic facsimiles of the real thing, they have no sense of community and identity . . . and most importantly, they don't give back to those who keep them successful.

I mean, did you ever try to put the arm on a neighborhood designer coffee stand? They tell you to contact the main office in Seattle where all the billing is handled . . . and then they want everything in triplicate and you have to wait in line for hours on some phone queue only to be told that there are no customer service representatives available (even though they have the whole subcontinent of India manning their phones).

It's just not worth it.

This is why Mario the Squid organized his take-back-the-neighborhood-business movement . . . because if the business isn't a real part of the neighborhood, then there is nothing left to take.

Momo's Police Assist

*N*ever make a mess in your own backyard, and if it is at all possible, make sure that no one else tries to, either.

Sam "Momo" Giancana took these words to heart.

There was a really nice and scenic park not too far from his home, just slightly north and west of Chicago.

Sam was no stranger to rough stuff and he was prone to party hearty with the best of them, but when it came time to call it a day and get some shut-eye, he just wanted to be free of hassles, kick back, and relax.

Unfortunately, this tranquil respite was soon interrupted by a police dragnet, as an unknown assailant was laying prey to young women in a nearby park. Much to the public's outrage, the police force was fairly ineffectual in their pursuit and capture of this menace to society.

This is not to say that there weren't enough officers assigned to the case—you couldn't throw a pair of dice without running into some of Chicago's finest in Sam's neighborhood, which, needless to say, really began to grate on his nerves.

After yet another unthwarted attack, Sam called in the cops and made a deal.

Pull back your dragnet for a week and let me handle it.

They did.

He did.

. . . and the attacks stopped, never to resume again.

Of course, on the record, the case remains unsolved . . . but who really cares about that?

Sam Giancana was instrumental in the removal of a recognized menace to society and restored the peace and tranquility to his suburban neighborhood.

What more could anyone ask?

The specifics and the who, how, and what really didn't matter.

Lucky's Patriotic Act

*W*hen it comes to homeland security, this thing of ours is a very necessary component.

In fact, one of the first heroes of homeland security, before the term was even coined, was none other than Charlie Lucky himself, Salvatore Lucania/Lucky Luciano.

Lucky was a great believer in protecting civilians. You just look him up in those FBI files that were released or those books *Bloodletters and Badmen* or *Murder, Inc.*, or even that online Wikipediz thing. He was the first modern mobster with businesses throughout the country. His longtime friend Meyer Lansky served as his right-hand man, and Luciano always followed Lansky's advice. During the years of Luciano's rule, he made this pact: "We only kill each other"; cops and civilians were hands-off.

In essence he was living the American dream in its truest form.

During World War II the U.S. government made

a deal with the at-that-time-imprisoned Luciano (convicted on trumped-up pandering charges by the soon-to-be failed politician Thomas Dewey). U.S. military intelligence knew Luciano maintained contact with certain relatives (one might say family members) thought to be associated with the Sicilian and Italian "organizations," which were none too happy about the way they were being treated by that brownshirt Mussolini, and the U.S. hoped to take advantage of them as part of the war effort. Lucky was a loyal American devoted to the land of his birth, this thing of ours, and the United States alike. And besides that, family always comes first. During the invasion of Italy, the U.S. used his "family" connections in Italy and Sicily to gather intelligence and help U.S. forces take over the Italian peninsula. Here at home, he helped prevent Nazi "interference" on U.S. shores. He made sure dockworkers didn't strike. He even used his "connections" to provide the U.S. with information on Communist influence on resistance groups and local governments.

. . . and in return for his patriotism, what did he receive after the war?

Parole . . . and deportation back to Sicily.

Thus ends a great American success story of homeland security.

See Something . . .
Say What?

. . . and speaking of homeland security . . .

Don Minestrone has no problem with the suggestion "if you see something, say something" . . . I mean, after all, we're all in this together.

My only problem is the question "to who?" as in "say something to who?"

Now, nobody likes a stoolie . . . so that rules out most of the cops.

(I mean, really—". . . but, officer, I didn't sell him the black-market semiautomatic weapons, so why do you want to know the names of all of my customers?")

And, of course, even among *our* friends some of us are less than discriminating in our choice of business partners (". . . but what do you mean I have to sell him the semiautomatic weapons so that you can sell him the ammunition?").

And, of course, no one wants to be accused of playing favorites, stealing from Gallo to give to Colombo, if you know what I mean.

Which is, of course, why the whole concept of "the neighborhood" is so important.

What's good for the neighborhood is what's good for America.

It's where you can nip the problems in the bud by staying on top of things.

On a one-to-one basis you know who you trust, you tell them and they will do the same, and the problem will get solved.

No red tape.

No hearings.

No finger-pointing.

Pre-emptive action works . . . particularly when only those involved know about it and their motives are pure (which pretty much rules out any of the pezzonovantes in D.C.).

Son of Sam

"Disco Carl," who used to be a semi-regular at that disco that Travolta did his "fever" at back in his younger years, always thought that it was more than a bit ironic that the so-called "Son of Sam" laws are constantly used against mobsters to try to thwart their book deals. Henry Hill, Sammy the Bull, you name it; they've all run into this obstacle on their way to literary greatness.

And, in reality, it's even more unfair since this thing of ours mobilized to protect the innocent during that legendary Summer of Sam.

To begin with, remember that killer was running around on our turf, killing our type of people who patronize our sort of clubs (not to say that the fall-off in patronage from fear was a real contributing factor; it wasn't).

Heck, Carmine Galante, sixty-seven, the nation's most powerful Mafia leader, personally ordered his men into the hunt when the boys in blue and the

Feds failed to make an impact. (Rupert Murdoch's *Post* originally reported that "the Mafia" had joined the hunt because the killings were hurting mob-controlled dating bars and discos, as if our own young guys and their lady friends weren't equally imperiled by the situation; by the way, they later backed away from that report when the Feds shot it down, not that they're any more credible than New York's favorite tabloid and birdcage liner.)

Just as we helped keep the peace during that summer's blackout, we lent a hand on the manhunt, though I must confess it was a parking ticket that brought him down and neither us nor the boys in blue were really responsible.

So when you think of Son of Sam and the mob, remember we did our part; don't think of that bogus law.

Accommodation Is Our Middle Name

*P*art of our stock-in-trade is the accommodation of those civilians who like to engage in what we like to call "victimless crimes."

A bet here and there, a "really subprime" loan to make it to the end of the month, a date for the socially challenged . . . you get the idea.

Accommodation is our middle name.

Out-of-state fireworks is another one of the services we like to provide—I mean, are kids in New York dumber or more accident-prone than some kid in the Ozarks? I don't think so.

The rockets' red glare and the bombs bursting in air are a necessary demonstration of our American heritage.

That's why the Dapper Don, Honest John Gotti, used to always put on a wonderful Fourth of July fireworks display/exhibition in his hometown of Howard Beach each year.

Made you proud to be an American and a distributor of fireworks as well.

A Melting-Pot Mob

$\mathcal{F}$or all of my talk about neighborhoods and this thing of ours, it is equally important to remember that, like America, we too are a melting pot, having taken in the world's tired, homeless, yadda yadda yadda. And like all good beneficiaries of the good graces of the folks at Ellis Island, we have prospered.

Not just Cosa Nostra . . . all of us.

Think about it for a minute.

What would Prohibition have been like without our good friends to the north who supplied us with Canadian whiskey?

Where would you find a good kneecapper if the Westies hadn't settled in Hell's Kitchen and the Bulgers in Boston?

And what about the entire numbers racket? I don't recall many Wall Street types pushing policy on 125th Street in the days before Lotto?

Not a Sicilian among them.

This thing of ours profits from the melting pot, as does all of America.

Brownstone Aerobics

*P*ark Slope Sal never left Brooklyn, and he wouldn't let his crew leave, either.

When other crews moved out to Long Island or relocated to the Southwest or, worse yet, Staten Island, Sal stayed put and made sure his guys did the same.

Sal believed in railroad flats and brownstones—street in front, yard in back, roofs shared by everyone on the block.

Nice, simple, and easy to defend (thanks to the lovely older ladies of the neighborhood who watched the streets night and day).

Say what you want about glass high-rises, ranch houses, and gated communities—Park Slope Sal wouldn't have it any other way.

And forget the elevators.

Sal spent his life living in a fifth-floor walkup even when he owned several other buildings, and he never regretted it.

No one has to waste time at the gym or jogging in Prospect Park when you live in a fifth-floor walkup . . . and the first guy in the crew who started to pant or breathe heavy on his way up those five flights of stairs was going to find his share of the take greatly curtailed.

The health plan in this thing of ours is almost as bad as most corporations, so Sal made sure that his crew was as healthy as a stable of fine thoroughbreds.

Who needs a StairMaster when you have a brownstone?

Getting Out the Vote

$\mathcal{T}$he best of our best in this thing of ours believe in America and its institutions.

(Okay, maybe not all of its institutions, but at least some of them.)

And as a result many of our number lend their support to the political process.

Now, I'm not talking about "buying elections."

That's a waste of money.

. . . but "get out the vote" programs are a different story.

The more people who vote, the more likely that an election will represent the will of the people rather than those of a chosen few.

Just like gambling, prostitution, and bootlegging, it has always been our business to provide the common man with access to those things that the nebulous, suited masters of money try to deny him.

I remember Sam G.'s extraordinary "get out the vote" campaign in Chicago that one year.

He made it so that the will of the people was truly heard.

. . . the dead as well as the living.

(Who's to say that breathing is a just requirement for suffrage?)

———◆◆◆———

Wasting time is always a bad thing, and right up at the top of the list is wasting the time of your attorney.

Remember, his job is to defend you, so either be honest with him or just keep your yap shut and let him do his work.

If you lie or engage in less-than-honest conversations with him, you are wasting both of your time.

And remember, he charges by the hour.

———◆◆◆———

On Taking Care of Business

A wiseguy's gotta do what a wiseguy's gotta do . . .
and nobody gets paid for doing nothin'.

———◆———

There is never too little time for bocce.

It's a great way to evaluate how your crew works together, how they communicate, what's their precision, and what is their focus.

For civilians it's just a lawn game; for our friends, it's an opportunity to be taken advantage of.

(And if you hold the balls just right it can block your mouth when you are speaking, which plays havoc with the Fed surveillance team that is trying to read your lips.)

———◆———

American Capitalism

*L*ucky Luciano was a shrewd judge of American capitalism.

He is quoted as saying, "There's no such thing as good money or bad money; there's just money," and "Ever since we was kids, we always knew that people can be bought; it was only a question of who did the buyin' and for how much."

In many ways, he was the first *real* supply-sider, or, in his own words, "If you have a lot of what people want and can't get, then you can supply the demand and shovel in the dough."

Online

*T*his online economy that all the kids are talking about is a pain in the butt.

One of my best earners, a hijacker by the moniker of Hyram Jack (no lie), tried to streamline our way of doing things by turning it over to this cyber whiz kid he called the Master.

The so-called Master told him that he didn't need a fence any longer and advised him to cut out the middleman and unload everything through eBay, whose cut was substantially less than even the most kindhearted fence and with whom Hy could conduct his business safely, without ever meeting the buyer or the facilitator.

Several of us old guys advised him against this new endeavor . . . but the sun rose and set on this little nerd in his eyes ever since he helped Hy Jr. get through NYU.

So the kid sets everything up for him, including quick and easy shipping and postage with scheduled pickups each week by the U.S. Postal Service.

In no time at all Hy is rolling in the dough and trying to win over more guys to his way of doing things.

Jack on Monday.

Inventory on Tuesday.

Posting on Wednesday.

Sale on Saturday.

Then it all fell apart.

First were the bills from the post office.

Then there were queries from New York state about uncollected sales tax.

. . . which of course led to further queries about unpaid income tax.

Hy needed help and he needed help fast—not to mention a good lawyer and a good accountant . . . but when he went to make a withdrawal from the account that his "earnings" were being directly deposited in, *nada!*

The account was empty . . . and the so-called Master was nowhere to be found.

Hy's now doing time upstate and rumor has it that the Master is running something called a MUD, where kids imagine themselves as organized-crime figures jockeying for control.

Don't ask me if it's any good . . . ask Hy; he lived it and lost.

Me . . . computers scare me, and they're going to stay that way.

The Commies

A lot of what we do is misconstrued.

Take our out-of-state cigarette importation program, whereby Donny the Snook drives south every other week to load up a truck with cigarettes that we distribute back home in the city at a substantial savings to the consumer, given the fact that we manage to avoid the state taxes and fees that have grown so huge over the years.

The way I look at it, smokers choose to smoke and, ergo, they can choose to do business with us.

Vice has always been a lucrative enterprise for our way of doing things.

Now, the Russkies try to do the same thing with gasoline . . . and that's just wrong. It's downright unpatriotic.

Gas taxes go to fix the roads and stuff, and driving is not a choice and, as a result, numerous civilians wind up involved in their criminal enterprises without any wrongdoing on their own part.

The only good thing about the Russkies is that with this whole out-of-state-gasoline thing, they manage to keep the IRS off our backs for a while.

After all, no one wants the commies to undermine our American way of life.

Right?

Flat World

*I*n the olden days we used to manage to make our displeasure known with certain corporate types through union actions and various "misadventures" that might get in the way of them conducting business.

But now in this "flat world" "service economy," where employees don't seem to have a voice, let alone access to an ear to listen to them, the terms "job action" just don't seem to have teeth anymore, particularly when that job is on its way to a desk in Bangalore.

As a result, we too must modernize our methods and hit them where it hurts.

Numbers Neal was a master at manipulating the new data economy and he never kept his money in the same account for more than forty-eight hours in any given week.

Hedge funds, money markets, sweep accounts, he knew it all, and more than that, people listened to him.

So if someone did something he didn't like, he'd call a few friends on a slow news day and engineer a few drastic sell-offs right before closing on a Friday or a three-day weekend close of business as a sort of warning shot, not unlike the rock through the plate glass window of yesteryear.

Almost always, the corporate types got the message.

Big Mouth Mario, on the other hand, had no head for numbers . . . but what he did know was the media, and the media knew him as well, frequently going to him for a typical "no comment" on any given mob matter . . . even those he knew nothing about.

Mario liked the attention.

He felt it gave him power . . . and it did.

When Mario didn't like what a certain corporation was doing, he'd make sure that he was seen prowling the hallways of their home office, or perhaps be overheard talking to Securities and Exchange Commission investigators about certain business affairs, or even just freely giving tips about this company because he felt that "they were in good hands" with access to the type of bare-knuckles influence that is needed for our current rough-and-tumble markets.

Corporations didn't like his sort of endorsements.

They led to a lot of scrutiny and large PR bills. . . . and the faster they got the message, the faster he would shut up.

One might say that sometimes a kind word is every bit as effective as a sledgehammer, and less taxing on the upper torso as well.

A Civil Union

*U*nion Sal was the son of Union Dom, who used to liaise with all of the city's civil service unions in matters pertaining to this business of ours. When Dom decided to retire to the sunny climes of Arizona, it was generally agreed upon that the "union duties" should be split among more individuals . . . but out of deference to Union Dom, Union Sal was given first choice of the finest, the bravest, the most reliable, etc.

And you know what he picked?

He picked the sanitation union.

When asked why, he replied, "I want to keep my hands clean."

And indeed he did.

Union Sal knew how to turn a profit by just making sure that the sanitation guys did their jobs.

No bribes, no pad, no nothing.

Now, of course, if a certain store owner needed a little encouragement to hire a private contractor for his refuse removal, a few visits and citations from enforcement agents (merely doing their jobs) often did the trick.

And if a certain garbage truck driver avoided traffic by changing his route and in doing so happened to accommodate some addresses earlier in the day than others, so be it.

And, of course, Sal was always there when they needed help in the usual type of things that unions were supposed to do.

And all the guys loved Sal, even more than his dad, because they knew that he had picked them over the Finest and the Bravest.

Nowhere was this ever clearer than when snow would fall on the Big Apple.

The trucks with their plows all had carefully mapped out routes and grids to follow as they performed the task of snow removal . . . but, funny thing, in order to get from the garages to their assignments, most of the G-Men (as Sal liked to call them) always wound up going down the streets where Sal, his family, and his friends resided.

On the Way Out

*S*ome guys think that outside of this thing of ours, their most important civilian associate is their lawyer.

They're wrong—it's their funeral director.

Think about it.

Your relationship is a two-way street.

He does a good job for you, you generate more business for him.

(Sometimes he can even give you a two-for-one special if you have an extra body hanging around that needs disposing of before it becomes offensively noticeable.)

And remember, he may not guarantee that you will make a good-looking corpse, but he will promise you that he will do his best.

Nice Vice

*S*al the Pal used to always say that just because the business was vice didn't mean you didn't have to be nice.

I remember that there was a certain lowlife pimp who used to take out his gambling losses on the girls in his stable . . . which is not to say that he ever made good on any of those gambling losses.

As it is with most lowlifes, eventually he had to be dealt with.

And he was, in a manner of great permanence.

Which led to the question, what are we going to do with the stable?

Sal had the answer.

As of recent he had been reading a lot of management books by guys with good American names like Iacocca, Machiavelli, and Trump.

Just because the upper reaches of management were bad was no reason to assume that the business itself was less than sound, and indeed it was the job of new management to assess the workforce and chart a new direction that would be beneficial to all parties concerned.

Once that was done, the new management had to present the new ideas to the employees and offer them the chance to join in the change of direction or leave on good terms.

Now, no self-respecting goodfella wants to be a pimp.

It's too much of a step down.

So no matter how you looked at it, business at the stable level was going to have to change, so one by one Sal interviewed the girls (plus a guy named Sharee . . . don't ask; you don't wanna know).

And you know what?

They liked the business they were in.

They just wanted a change of scenery and clientele.

So some went to Jersey.

Some went to Vegas.

And some went to D.C.

And as a result, Sal made friends all over the country.

The Gyp

*M*orrie the Gyp had been busted by the best, if you were to believe everything he said.

If you had a book out about what you did, he'd point to a given page and say, "That was me."

He'd been busted on cases related to Henry Hill and Sammy "The Bull" Gravano.

He'd been fingered by info from Pistone and Leuci, and he even claimed to have been ticketed by the SuperCops Greenberg and Hantz.

He also liked to claim that he was busted by Frank Serpico but that the collar had been re-allocated to someone else.

Hill and Gravano, he acknowledged, were rats, but the cops, they were just doing their jobs.

Just as Charlie Lucky treated cops as "hands off," Morrie the Gyp saw them as a necessary evil.

"If they catch me or someone who is stealing from me, either way, they are doing their job, so what right do I have to complain?"

His understanding and grace, however, never extended as far as the meter maids and traffic cops. "They're just wasting my time, the pikers. Why spend the day giving out tickets when there are guys like me walking the streets? I'm not gonna respect you unless you're going after the best with both barrels fully loaded. An expired meter? Don't waste my time."

Vig Advice

*M*an does not live by vig alone.

Contrary to popular belief, you can get blood from a stone . . . but once you've done that, whatta you got?

A bloody stone, that's what.

Which is why the vig a man is really expected to pay should never exceed his true earning potential.

Men with empty pockets never pay their debts, nor do they try to make other arrangements that might be mutually beneficial.

Make sure that the vig never wipes them out.

Don't use it as the mace to bash their skulls in . . . use it as the ball and chain to train a new hound.

In the end, the final accounting will always be most advantageous.

Remember to keep yourself up-to-date with your Lord and Maker.

The vig is a bitch if it's not paid off when your time is due.

On $\mathcal{B}$usiness $\mathcal{E}$thics

Unlike the corporate world, life in this thing of ours does not require that we divorce "Family values" from "business ethics" . . . and unlike our civilian counterparts, we actually understand the implications and consequences of both.

———◆◆◆———

Joe Stassi's words to the wise:

"Always empty a gun before you toss it. Someone finds an empty gun, they're likely to keep it or sell it. If they find a partially empty gun, they'll turn it in to the cops for fear of being connected with whoever got shot" . . . and no one wants that to happen.

———◆◆◆———

Money in the Pocket

*I*t's a well-known fact that people need walking around money.

It's, how they say, an integral component of their self-worth.

This is true for wiseguys and civilians alike and is also one of the reasons why I personally can't stand muggers.

Now, I'm not saying that an occasional civilian doesn't get strong-armed into coming across with some cash unexpectedly.

Business is business, after all.

I'm just saying that at least most of the wise-guys I know try to stay away from unknowns . . . particularly civilians.

Quite frankly, some old lady's Social Security check just ain't worth it.

And that's the problem with muggers . . . what they get for what they do just ain't worth it.

Not for them, and definitely not for the victim.

This is why my crew keeps an eye on everything that happens in the neighborhood, and keeps an ear out for these types of occurrences (and, of course, most of the old folks around here know they can just come by the old social club if something needs to be brought to our attention).

As a result, muggers are dealt with quickly and efficiently.

They stop and channel their energies otherwise or they go away, if not by their own volition then by some lasting encouragement from some of my guys.

Steal from the Insured

$\mathcal{G}$enie the Judge, who used to boost cars in upstate New York, shared some valuable insight with me on the auto trade:

Always steal the most expensive car available.

Why, you ask?

Those are the cars that are most likely owned by people with either the best insurance or the least dependence on their vehicle for their day-to-day survival.

After all, heisting cars isn't personal, so if possible, inconvenience only the people who are best equipped to deal with the outcome.

And if possible, get the ones with the MD plates. Not only do cops shy away from ticketing them, you can usually park 'em anywhere.

Leftover Plates

$\mathcal{G}$enie the Judge also had some other advice on car heisting:

If it's at all possible, ditch the license plates of the vehicle on the spot (unless they're MD, as I previously mentioned).

It's bad enough the guy has to get a new car—that's just the price of doing business—but having to wait in line at the Motor Vehicle Bureau to take care of the old, "missing" plates while filing for a new set? No one deserves that.

Leaving them where they parked the car gives them a fighting chance to avoid that pure hell of municipal procedure.

(But remember to always wipe off your prints from the plates first—and if you can't remember to do that, forget about what I just said. A civilian's inconvenience is not worth your possible jail time.)

A Last Meal

I remember hearing the story of how Benny the Food Fence made his bones.

Benny didn't just deal food, he prepared it like a gourmet. When you went to the mattresses you wanted to hole up with Benny for some really good eats.

Benny once got a call from Tony the Wop, who was his boss.

Tony had a very sad duty to perform . . . he had to take out one of his oldest and dearest friends who, rumor had it, was thinking of turning state's evidence.

Benny knew the guy and offered to cook him a farewell meal.

Tony said sure, knowing full well that his friend would never turn down a Benny feast and what more perfect way to set up the hit.

So Benny makes the meal and serves Tony and the target.

Minutes later the target is gasping for breath and dies on the spot. No blood, no nothin'.

Turns out the guy was highly allergic to shellfish, which Benny coincidentally used in the stock he used to flavor the pasta.

Whether Benny knew about this aforementioned condition is debatable . . . but he did save Tony the trouble and agita of offing his oldest friend.

ID DOA

*J*ackie the Shiv was a family man.

He knew what it was like to worry about a missing loved one. His brother was missing for nine months before his body turned up. He would have wound up in Potter's Field had the eagle eye of a morgue attendant not recognized a birthmark on his *tukkes* (they had been in gym together back in the day).

That's why whenever Jackie made a hit up close he always slapped a HELLO, MY NAME IS_____ sticker on the body before dumping it. Even after the scavengers cleaned out his pockets of ID, the deceased was still clearly labeled so that loved ones could be contacted.

Scalped

$\mathcal{T}$ix the Scalper could get his hands on tickets for any event . . . at a price, of course.

Over his career, he secured primo seats for the Rat Pack Reunion at the Sands, the Ali-Frazier fight, Madonna doing that Mamet thing on Broadway, even the pope's gig at Yankee Stadium. . . . If you needed a ticket, Tix was your man.

Tix had the connections and he made you pay, but he never judged you.

Not when Joey G. asked him for Met Opera tickets, nor when Harry H. asked him for Red Sox seats behind the dugout.

He also conveniently forgot what you ordered before if anyone inquired ("No, can't say I recall getting Streisand or Minnelli tickets for anyone on your crew"), yet always remembered to tip you off to something he thought was up your alley that had just become available ("I understand there's a road company of *La Cage* in Vermont that's being headlined by Jon Stewart and Stephen Colbert. Interested?").

Only once did he wind up brokering *fugazis* . . . and not only did he make good on them with interest, he threw in a pair of Super Bowl boxes gratis.

The guy who passed him the fugazis didn't make out as well.

Tix called in Tony the Injun, and he gave the rat a lesson in a different type of scalping that was a lesson to anyone else who thought they could pull one over on the true Ticketmaster of the five boroughs.

———◆◆◆———

A loud gun is always the best.

It scares the civilians, gets them out of your way, and cuts down on what you call collateral damage.

Nobody gets paid extra for unnecessary downed targets.

———◆◆◆———

On Career Advice

For some guys a job is just a paycheck.
For others it's a stepping stone in a career.
For wiseguys it's a part of your life, finito, no
questions asked, no answers volunteered.
No regrets.

What He Deserves

*F*rankie the Eel was one of those really shortsighted guys who was always trying to make the short buck . . . just enough to cover his nut plus enough to kick upstairs without ever raising anyone's expectations.

. . . and Madonna forbid he felt that you were trying to chisel him.

Not that you would have anything to worry about physically . . . unless, of course, you counted your ears, which would be burning as he whined to everyone he came in contact with about how you had done him wrong and chiseled him out of his hard-earned cash.

No injustice was ever so slight that it couldn't be blown up to something the size of the Knapp Commission.

Things got so bad that Big Paulie, who was married to Frankie's sister, finally had to have a sit-down with everyone.

Bottom line—Paulie was sick and tired of being a listener on the Frankie the Eel party line of complaints . . . and it had better stop soon.

Frankie read this meeting as "everyone better give him what he deserved" and left with a self-satisfied grin of Sicilian smugness.

Everyone else read this as "someone better give him what he deserved," and that someone was Little Paulie, who was married to Big Paulie's sister.

Little Paulie approached the Eel, who immediately turned around to confront him, saying, "You heard what Big Paulie said, and as I recall you owe me a deuce. Now pay up!"

So Little Paulie gave him exactly what he deserved.

He then informed him that everyone else would do the same should the situation arise again.

The Eel didn't do much talking for the next three months, as his broken jaw was slow to heal . . . and even after that no one heard as much from him, as he decided that it might be better to keep his complaints to himself.

Vanity Plates

$\mathcal{F}$or a while there, vanity license plates were a big thing among some of the newer wiseguys. Some of them even spent A-1 favors with city and state types to lock in their moniker of choice on their vehicles' tags.

In no time at all, guys were driving around with tags that read:

WYZGUY

GDFTHR

HITMAN

BOOSTER

HI-JACK

and even

CAPONE

LUCIANO

CORLEONE

and

DPPRDON

Some guys even acquired other guys' tags in exchange for unpaid vig or unwanted injury.

These guys saw their tags as a matter of pride and prestige, and they were all riding high on their self-importance.

But in the words of Philosopher Frank, "Pride always cometh before a fall" and "Vanity is the quicksand of reason." Such memorable monikers seem to have gotten in the way of clear thinking.

So when Georgie Boy Digeorgio made his first six-figure score, his captain, Marco the Pole, offered him his own choice of vanity plates as a sort of graduation present as he entered the ranks of major earners.

Georgie Boy was touched, thought about it for a moment, and asked for plate number 1111.

Captain Marco, a man of his word, said, "Sure, but what does it mean?"

"Nothing," Georgie Boy replied, "but with four small pieces of tape, my tags will be unrecognizable and discreet after dark, 'cause, y'know, being memorable and distinct is not exactly helpful in our line of work."

Captain Marco agreed . . . and within two weeks vanity plates disappeared from the vehicles of everyone on his crew, but not before he got wind of an all-points bulletin BOLO (be on the lookout) for a getaway car with the plates BADABING.

On-the-Mark Advice

*W*illie the Man (short for Willie the Marksman) always said that you need to take pride in your work without succumbing to the sin of pride.

You go in, you do the job, and you get out and be on your way.

Now, this is not to say that you rush things.

Bang bang . . . you bring him down.

Blam blam blam blam . . . you make sure that he's not going to get up.

. . . and you get out of there confident and proud of a job well done.

Game over.

What you don't do is stick around and admire your handiwork on the spot (you can always check out the police photos in the tabloids the next day) or steal a peek at the crowd, feasting off their fear and awe.

Remember, there is no statute of limitations on murder, and standing around like a statue at the scene of the crime is one of the surest ways to guarantee you'll be confronting those charges at some time in your future . . . and who wants to railroad a promising career with a silly little error of judgment like that?

The Habitual Crime

$\mathcal{D}$onald Westlake is a funny writer.

He's not a wiseguy, but he is a man deserving of respect.

His book *The Hot Rock* is one of the funniest crime stories I've ever read, and I will always hold the memory of reading it in a special place in my heart (and not just because I was reading it to pass the time as my mouthpiece was springing me for something I actually was guilty of).

It has to do with a heist that keeps going wrong, so the perps have to keep swiping the swag again and again.

It's a bunch of habitual criminals involved in a truly habitual crime.

That story reminds me of the story of Burt the Bouncer and his unlucky ill-gotten gain.

Burt hired himself out as a sort of freelance bouncer.

If you had a problem at your club or thought that there might be potential for some ugliness, you might hire Burt to hang out for a while and lend a hand.

In return Burt drew a deuce from the till, drank for free, and helped himself to the pickings from anyone he had to remove.

After the removal, Burt would be on his way, immediately forgotten by club clientele and management alike.

After a lucrative assignment, Burt surveyed his takings and handed them over to a fence for a quick negotiation.

Satisfied with the price, he was counting his payment when he noticed an inscription on the back of the gold Rolex he had appropriated: TO MICKEY FROM MANXIE.

All night he couldn't get it out of his head.

Then it dawned on him.

Uh-oh.

TO MICKEY FROM MANXIE.

Mickey was Don Mancini's godson, and Manxie was Mickey's wife.

Burt tried to remember what the guy looked like, but the club was dark and it was all fairly routine, so he really hadn't been paying attention.

He figured he'd better get the watch back—fast.

Breaking in to the fence's shop was easy.

Locating the watch was easier.

Getting hit over the head by an unnamed intruder was easiest of all.

Coming around watch-less ten minutes later was, however, a bitter pill to swallow.

A shower and a McMuffin later, Burt's pager buzzed.

The Man Upstairs wanted to see him.

Don Mancini greeted him with concern. "You look like crap."

"You should see the other guy."

"I did," he replied.

"You did?"

"Yeah . . . he ain't coming around here no more. Here's your wallet. He's in the bay now."

Burt was puzzled.

"For stealing my wallet?"

"Nah," the don replied, "for sleeping with my godson's wife. She even gave him Mickey's watch, if you can believe that. Now Mickey's got his watch back, she got a lesson in the wages of infidelity, and the no-good *gafone* got an up-close view of the East River."

Manxie never cheated on Mickey again (at least not that he found out), and the guy that Burt had beat up thought that it would be better if he relocated to the West Coast.

And the next time Burt laid claim to his pickings he always took a piece of ID as well, as you never know whose pocket you might be picking.

The Face of . . .

*S*ome guys get really hung up on things, which is why I always tell my shooters, hit the target, confirm the kill, and leave.

Don't stand around looking for details; that's the job of some scene director in the film version.

There's nothing to be gained looking at pools of blood.

Matty the Hammer once thought he saw the face of God in the blood spatters, and he swore off any more hits until he realized that what he really saw was the reflection of a poster of Al Pacino as Serpico in the pool of blood.

That point realized, he was back at work in no time.

Honest Theft

Somebody once said, "An educated man can steal more with a fountain pen than with a handgun," and when I look at some of these CEOs with their seven-figure pensions for life while their employees wind up squeaking by on Social Security and cat food, well, it just burns me up.

There is something blatantly dishonest about that way of life.

Rewards should require an element of risk, but those guys aren't just shooting craps with loaded dice; they're cashing in their chips and counting their winnings without ever sitting down and playing.

That's worse than cheating.

Nobody should be rewarded for just showing up.

Give me a .45 instead of a fountain pen any day.

I am a man of honor, after all.

Always know who you are really working for.

That nice little bonus you hijacked along the way won't count for much if it was part of the black-market fugazis your captain had just secured.

No one likes their pocket picked, even when you're planning to refill it.

On "The Family"

It's the most important thing . . .
and you don't talk about it.

Never bet against the Family.

. . . unless someone discreet is willing to give you really good odds.

Contrary to popular belief, not everyone loves a winner.

. . . but everyone does love winning.

Valachi

I know some guys who still spit on the ground every time they hear the name Joe Valachi.

They just can't stand to hear him mentioned . . . not that he was the first guy to ever squeal about our affairs, just the way he did it was what people had a problem with.

It wasn't the book deal (pretty neat piece of fiction) or the Charles Bronson movie (and, believe me, Valachi was a lot closer in appearance to Charles Durning than to Charles Bronson) . . . it was the way he weaseled around his own crimes.

"I admit to all of my criminal activities and acknowledge my guilt . . . but let the record show I never killed anyone. I'm not a murderer; I was just the driver and a good soldier."

Valachi was the same type of songbird as your current Britney Spears or Justin Timberlake— the perfect product of intense studio enhancement and PR.

. . . and when it comes right down to it, what do we remember him for?

For being a stool pigeon, which is roughly the equivalent of being remembered as the opening act for the New Kids on the Block reunion tour.

The Club

*W*hen civilians hear about "the club" as a mob hangout . . . they usually think of some big titty bar like the Bada Bing or maybe Scores . . . y'know, noisy, crowded, the type of place where you can run up a tab while just looking around.

That's not a club.

A club is a neighborhood place; it's a back room where the crew can gather and talk but also where people who want to find you can.

. . . and because it's in the neighborhood the rules are different than you would expect.

You don't have to be one of us . . . but you definitely have to belong there.

Mrs. Manicotti, salt of the earth and pure of soul, is always welcome to drop by, sometimes just to wink and say, "I read the headlines of yesterday's *Post* . . . I'll say an extra novena for you this week"; sometimes to drop off a tray of ziti. She stops by, says her piece, she leaves.

And she knows enough to read the crowd outside to determine if this is a good day to drop, or not.

Now, no one is ever going to give Mrs. Manicotti a hard time (and if someone did they would be answering to Tony the Zip before the local news-radio station had its next thrice-hourly weather update), but she knows that sometimes things go on that she doesn't want to know about.

That's why wives don't come by the club or girlfriends, either . . . and why a designated civilian always answers the phone, taking the message and letting the caller know that the person isn't present right now even when they are listening in on the other extension.

You got a problem, you let them know at the club.

You want to head off a problem, you let them know at the club.

You want to personally settle a problem in a manner that will be irreversible and as permanent as those paintings on the Vatican ceilings . . . then you do it as far away from the club as possible.

Hunting, fishing, sporting, shooting . . . who cares what type of club it's supposed to be.

It's what we are and what we do that is most important (and serious things like that don't usually happen around scantily clad dancers).

School

$\mathcal{T}$here is a common misconception that prison is a school for criminals in that by going there, you are taught to be a better criminal.

This is bunk.

You go to prison because you didn't learn your lessons—you blew it, you made a stupid mistake.

Prison is not Wiseguy U.

Sure, lowlifes like muggers, pushers, and punks can learn a few tricks in the big house—but that's strictly blue-collar stuff.

Our guys are professionals.

All of that said, sometimes a young guy needs to be taught a few lessons, and a few armed guards have been known to encourage better study habits.

Little Anthony, no relation to the singer, came from a really broken home (his dad drank too much and one day his mother took an ax to the apartment and the old man), but he was a whiz at numbers.

He could count cards with a six-deck shoe.

He could keep the odds for ten races in his head, all at the same time.

. . . and he could calculate interest compounded daily without a computer, calculator, or pen and pad.

He was a real numbers whiz.

. . . and he was only fourteen.

Problem was he was an undisciplined troublemaker (the type of kid my nana used to call a wild child) and he was almost illiterate, having dropped out of school around the time his mother was carted off to the state pen for her hatchet job on his father.

The kid could be a huge asset to an outfit . . . but only if he straightened up and flew right.

Now, normally when you have a kid with potential, you shield him from the law, but the big man upstairs decided on a different course of action. The first time Little Anthony got nicked, the man lined him up a fancy lawyer who kept him out of the reformatory and the social system and into a nice military academy where he served a four-year stint that yielded him not just a GED but a New York State Regents diploma as well.

For Little Anthony it might have been harder than a prison sentence . . . but in the end it all paid off for all concerned.

He was welcomed into this thing of ours and has become a useful and productive member of society as well.

His rewards were bigger than you would have expected for a punk like him before the big man intervened, and Little Anthony knows it.

And out of respect he does the big man's taxes every year . . . and whatever other numerical problems that come his way.

Respect and Short Arms

*R*espect is a big part of this thing of ours . . . but sometimes we forget it needs to flow both ways.

Take the case of Tony Short Arms.

It has more or less become a tradition that it is up to the lowest man in the hierarchy present at a given occasion to settle the bill . . . which means if you're the little guy in the group, you pay.

Now, part of this is related to where you're eating, part of it is related to who's there at what time, and part of it is related to whatever the big man wants to relate it to.

Now, Tony Short Arms got his nickname because even when in a group composed of his equals, he never picked up the check.

Sometimes he remembered an urgent call that required his attention.

Sometimes he fortuitously answered a call of nature.

. . . and sometimes he just picked a fight with the waiter or manager or whatever and the bill never got paid.

To all apparent observers, Tony Short Arms seemed incapable of picking up a check, and he'd always maneuver the situation in such a way that no one could claim that he was showing any disrespect and, as a result, no one ever called him on it.

Then one day word got around to the big man upstairs that Tony was disrespecting his own crew, bleeding them dry with his mealtime demands for fealty. In this particular case, the man upstairs heard about one of his favorite godsons, who was called in at the last minute at a meal for ten to share in the cannoli for dessert and as a result of five minutes at the table, got stuck with a bill for three Gs.

After further inquiry on his part, the big man upstairs determined that this was fairly routine for Tony and, as a result, he decided that it was time for Mr. Short Arms to partake in a little just desserts.

The first thing the big man upstairs did was make sure that Tony heard about the cuisine at a new Bensonhurst bistro . . . and once he did, the man upstairs sat back and watched.

Sure enough, Tony called together his crew and called a meeting at the place, which was of course none too cheap. Unbeknownst to him, his party for ten was soon going to be quite larger.

On the day of the dining, Tony and his crew showed up for the reservation, but before they could be seated, the big man upstairs caught Tony's eye and beckoned him over.

As "luck" would have it, the big man was also enjoying the cuisine du jour and insisted that Tony and his crew join them.

Tony, knowing that an offer he couldn't refuse had been made, graciously agreed and filled in the rest of the banquet table with his crew . . . one big, happy family.

The big man ordered the best for everyone and a menu was never seen.

Tony realized that he was low man in the big man's group and was exceptionally happy that his crew was also along to pick up the tab.

Now, the big man was the big man and what he said went, no matter who you were or what you were doing. So if he needed his laundry picked up at a certain time and he wanted one of your guys to do it, they did. If he needed someone to haul out to

Jersey to pick up his mother-in-law, they went . . . and that was that.

But as the sumptuous feast went on, Tony began to notice that his crew was being assigned to duties at an alarming rate, so that by the time espresso was being served, Tony was all alone with no one below.

What Tony was completely unprepared for was when the big man sent everyone else away so he could have a word with Tony.

. . . but first the big man informed the waiter that a golden-age-club gathering would also be added to the tab (friends of his mother who were dining at the same time) as well as a bottle of the house's best champagne for a cute pair of lovers sharing a cannoli (since we all remember what it was like to be young and in love), and also let the waiter add a 25 percent tip to the bottom for the wonderful service all had enjoyed that day.

Tony instantly knew what he had to do—he couldn't stiff the big man; he had to therefore stiff the bistro.

Get the check and leave . . . and if anyone tried to stop him, he'd just pull a Joe Pesci on him like in *Goodfellas* ("Put it on my tab," then never pay).

Unfortunately for Tony Short Arms, this was not to come to pass, because the big man's last words to him were: "I like this place. My brother-in-law has done a nice job of it. He and I are very close. We need to support more neighborhood establishments like this . . . make sure that they don't have any problems with check-beaters or other lowlifes."

With that, the big man left, and Tony Short Arms was soon on the phone with his local shylock for a high-interest influx of cash on the spot to pay the bill.

The next day, the big man gave Tony a call and said that he had enjoyed their meal together and that they should do it more often.

Tony agreed but mentioned that he was thinking of dieting for a while and might be skipping eating out for a bit.

The big man hung up with a smile, convinced that the lesson had been learned.

Hitting the Mattresses

*J*oey the Hitman, in his memoir (appropriately titled *Joey the Hitman: The Autobiography of a Mafia Killer*), went on record with the insight:

"Gang wars are about as much fun as walking through a plate glass window. There is no excitement, no adventure, only a lot of time laying low."

But not wanting to dispute my esteemed colleague's observation, "going to the mattresses," as we used to call it, had a tremendous upside as well.

Long before *Iron John* and *Fire in the Belly* and other classics of the so-called men's movement (where suburban guys would dance around fires and stuff to exert their manhood—no, I never got what they were supposed to be doing, either), lamming it was the time men could be around men without any interruption of home and/or domestic concerns.

The close quarters would bring us all together and help us to get to know each other a bit better.

You found out that Fat Tony snored and Greasy Tom needed a new deodorant and Danny the Dresser had probably never been with a girl in his life (and didn't seem to mind it one bit—it is what it is) and that Billy the Batter was a closet Red Sox fan . . . all that little stuff that you never really picked up on during the normal course of this thing of ours.

You also found out who you could really count on to think ahead about whether it was the right time to call for takeout (off hours) or the right time to change hide-outs (preferably some time before the cops came by with a warrant or a couple of goons dropped in with a shotgun and some heaters).

Priests and altar boys went on retreats . . . well, so did we, though usually not out of choice and with a timing determined by others (either above us or against us).

"Hitting the mattresses" was also the time to really indoctrinate any new guys—make them do the laundry, learn to cook, clean up, but also teach them a thing or two about making marinara for twenty, keeping one's cool, and cleaning one's weapon.

Some of my best memories were during those days when Joey Gallo was trying to make a name for himself.

Never would I have realized that laying low to stay alive would have been one of the most inspiring times of my life.

By Bread Alone

*A*nd one more lesson about hitting the mattresses: you can never make too much pasta or have too much marinara.

On the pasta, there's nothing better than a little carb-loading before a shoot-out or ambush.

It's also perfect for any meal—breakfast, lunch, or dinner (guys just don't care).

And marinara keeps.

Just heat it up and add some meat or veggies and you're good to go.

Man cannot live by bread alone.

. . . but some pasta and marinara and he's got a real shot.

New Words for Old

With all of this talk of the world being flat and that the economy is now global, things keep getting redefined in such a way that nothing is the same as it used to be.

(Frankie Widemouth slapped his daughter across the mouth and threatened to have her locked in a convent when she told him that she was working nights while training for a career in the service industry; he thought he had raised her better than that. Was he ever relieved when she landed at American Express in their customer service department.)

It's gotten so that our way of life has become lumped in with those of a bunch of miscreants.

There really is a difference between gangsters and "gangstas," and we were here first (and besides that, we know how to talk English real good so that everyone can understand us, and we know how to hold our pants up so that our underwear isn't showing, too).

Lumping us in with them is like calling a Sicilian a Corsican—no one gets away with it twice.

Sometimes they even lump bikers and outlaws in with us.

There was a book a few years back with the misleading title *Mafia Enforcer;* what was it about—a Luca Brasi type? Maybe a Frank Nitti? Of course not; it was about an undercover Hell's Angel sort of guy.

Talk about misleading.

And now there's talk that in reality there aren't five families, but instead there are six and one of them is Canadian?

What is this world coming to?

It tends to put the old guys into deep manicotti . . . but Philly the Kid (now in his eighties) remembers a time when every goodfella worth his salt knew Italian and could trace his family lineage back to the old country.

Times change and you have to roll with the punches.

Philly learned that lesson when his wife of forty years passed away.

He took up with a twenty-year-old Goth chick trying to make it off-Broadway.

He's never been happier and has embraced the mantra of "Change is good."

A Menu That Never Goes Out of Style

*M*ergers and acquisitions are tough on everyone, so a little understanding and sensitivity is a prerequisite.

It isn't always a crew's fault that they were taking orders from some real jerk that you successfully sent on a Jacques Cousteau training mission with concrete flippers.

Now this jerk's crew is your responsibility.

You need to see if they fit in, deal with possible redundancies of interest and influence, and, of course, gauge their individual loyalty and trustworthiness . . . all the normal, run-of-the-mill sort of things that need to be done after a major merger or acquisition.

The only problem is that in this thing of ours there is no room for a human resources department with nanny duties for the new hires.

We need to work out those things on our own.

Sometimes things work out fine.

Your target last week might be your triggerman this week.

Likewise, last week's employee of the year might be headed for his final sit-down this week if he can't get with the program and set old grudges aside.

Carlo the Chairman always used to have a nice lunch for his new hires, and usually by dessert he knew who would not be agreeing with him—sort of like a week-old stromboli.

"The way I look at things," he would say, "our business is like a really good neighborhood restaurant, sort of like New Corners in Bensonhurst. Occasionally you add new specials, some variations here and there, but mostly you keep the menu the same . . . it's why everybody keeps coming back. If a new special doesn't work out, it gets dropped. Likewise, if a new dish replaces an old dish, so be it, and it gets done with as little fanfare as possible.

"Spaghetti and meatballs never goes out of style, and when you have to choose *whose* spaghetti and meatballs you want, the answer is simple—the one that is the best.

"Those who work out stick around for coffee and cake, those who don't are dealt with *espresso*."

Remember, marinara goes with murder.

It helps to explain the stains if things get messy.

(No reason to unduly stress out those who are responsible for the laundry.)

On Lessons from Life and Wisdom

---

*I've lived a long time, not an easy thing
for someone in my line of work.*

Your Rep

*Y*our rep is only as good as the word of mouth that drives it.

A few words in the wrong ear—you're busted.

Too many words in the right ear—you're feared, but maybe plugged before you get out of hand.

Unlike other lines of work, we don't have the luxury of hiring spinmeisters and PR flacks for our day-to-day operations.

That type of thing is only good for civilian operations.

That's why it is important to locate whoever is the eyes and ears for the big man upstairs.

Sometimes it's his grocer.

Sometimes it's his driver.

. . . and sometimes it's the blind guy at the newsstand who seems to know the color of your tie just by talking to you.

Whoever it is, he is the guy you need to keep informed.

Word of mouth alone won't do it.

It's the mouth from which those words emerge that is the most important part of all.

The Way You Look

Looks and personal appearance are important.

Whether we like it or not, the odds are that at some point in our careers we will wind up with our pictures in the paper, and for most civilians this is the only snapshot of us they will ever see, so we owe it to ourselves to always look good and presentable.

Remember, a thug who looks like a thug looks like a convict. It's a sort of self-fulfilling sort of prophecy, an unfortunate societal sort of leap to definition.

"He looks like he belongs in jail, so let's send him to jail."

Now, a guy decked out in a nice well-cut suit (*not pimped out,* need I say) with a smile on his face—well, I'm sure there must have been some sort of mistake here because that man couldn't possibly be a criminal.

. . . and the smile is important.

It conveys confidence and affability.

It says, "Hey, you're just doing your job, so let's get this thing over so I can get out of here so that I can take my mother-in-law to her podiatrist."

John Gotti knew how to dress sharp . . . that's why he was called the Dapper Don.

And in his mug shot he always had a smile on his face . . . even when the no-good DA was railroading the case against him.

Healthy Food

*R*osario Cardelini got a bit paranoid and hypochondriacal in his later years.

He refused to listen to his lieutenants and he refused to consult his doctor.

He also refused to eat out . . . at all.

No more patronizing neighborhood haunts.

No more fast food.

No more takeout.

From the day he turned fifty-five, he only ate the food he grew in his own garden.

He got the idea for this from watching that sex and violence show on Channel 13 [ed. note: *I, Claudius* on Masterpiece Theatre] where the aging boss in the bathrobe and sheet wraparound only ate the fruits and vegetables that he picked from his own garden.

For two solid years we had to listen to how healthy his diet was—fish he kept alive and under observation in his pond until it was ready for the pot, beans galore, oatmeal, and lotsa spinach—spinach leaves, spinach soup, and even spinach pasta.

Nobody was going to poison him and he wasn't going to poison his own body by filling it with unhealthy toxins.

So what happened?

His big toe began to bother him . . . and it swelled up like an angry red balloon.

He never recalled feeling such pain before (it was even worse than the time he asked Jamie Garbo about his shrink and Jamie practiced his weekly two-fisted therapy session on him in return).

What was the cause?

Why, his healthy diet, of course!

Turns out too much of a good thing (spinach, fish, beans, etc.) can lead to a very bad thing: gout.

A physician or a nutritionist could have told him that.

Money Well-Spent

*I*t's never too late to do some community outreach.

At least that is what Silky Sy used to say.

Silky was part of the Jewish mob out of Jersey who used to come by the social club each year on his way to the San Gennaro festival.

"The thing is," he used to say, "is everybody likes a regular guy. Now, being respected is important but not always. Sometimes you need some sympathy, some empathy, some of that 'hey, that guy is just like me—why don't I lend him a hand' sort of stuff."

Take the case of Arthur Flegenheimer, or as he is better known, Dutch Schultz.

The Feds had the Dutchman in the same sort of bind as Capone—tax evasion—but they just couldn't make the case.

Why, you ask?

Well, where Capone was a clotheshorse, Schultz was, how shall I say, more casual.

You looked at Capone and you saw on his back more than you made the last three years.

Schultz, on the other hand, embraced frugality in his wardrobe. He claimed he never spent more than $35 or so for a suit or more than $2 for a shirt, and was quoted by the press as saying that "only a sucker will pay $15 or $20 for a silk shirt." (Charlie "Lucky" Luciano confirmed this, going on the record saying, "Schultz was one of the cheapest guys I ever knew, practically a miser. Here was a guy with a couple of million bucks and he dressed like a pig. He used to brag that he never spent more than thirty-five bucks for a suit, and it hadda have two pairs of pants.")

But that which might appear to be "cheap" or slovenly to the Park Avenue set was easily accepted by the average working guy who didn't have a cent to spare on fashion or accessories.

When it came time for his trial, his attorneys managed to secure a change of venue out of the sin city of the five boroughs and up to the virtuous pastures of upstate New York, where Schultz pressed his side of the disagreement to the public. He claimed that he was just a victim of bad accounting advice and that once he found out that he was misinformed: "I offered $100,000 when the government was broke and people were talking revolution and they turned me down cold. You can see how that at least I was willing to pay. Everybody knows that I am being persecuted in this case. I want to pay. They were taking it from everybody else, but they wouldn't take it from me. I tried to do my duty as a citizen. . . ."

And given the complexities of the tax code, more people than not were easily convinced that there was a sufficient degree of reasonable doubt to grant him an out on the "honest mistake" defense.

In fact, the regular folk who made up the jury had gotten to know Schultz before the trial.

To them he was not just some mobster out of the headlines. He was the guy who came by to get to know everyone a few days back. He bought everyone a few rounds at the local tavern, attending a few local sporting events, tipped his hat to the ladies . . . everything you would expect from a regular guy.

Schultz had earned from them a different type of respect; the type they felt towards each other . . . and in doing so, unlike Capone, he also earned himself an acquittal.

Fugazis

*F*ugazis are never for family.

Girlfriends and gumares, sure.

. . . but never family.

For a wife, a mother, or a daughter, it doesn't have to be showy—it just has to be real.

Their love for you is worth more than mere jewelry, and they deserve the best (and in a tight spot they will always be willing to hock it for your ransom or a lawyer's legal retainer).

Anyone who passes fugazis to you as if they were the real thing doesn't love or respect you (or, just perhaps, they might be too stupid or hapless to actually recognize the difference between what they have and the real thing).

Either way, you know that you can't count on them.

Passing off fakery for the real thing is not an endearing trait.

Which is not to say that you shouldn't do business with them.

Things are what they are.

You just need to go in with your eyes wide open and knowledgeable enough to know a fugazi when you see it.

Friends

*F*riends who remain friends for over forty years are true friends.

I remember back when we were wet behind the ears.

What blowhards we were.

It wasn't enough that you made your bones; you had to share it with everyone else.

And it wasn't just "Well, I did it. Today I am a made man."

It was a second-by-second recap of everything that went on, kinda like that fat guy's movie on the president reading that kid's book when the Arabs attacked the towers . . . every little movement you noticed as each second ticked by.

It was almost like being there.

By his side as he made his bones.

Sharing in the experience.

This sharing of ego even covered the day-to-day stuff, the kneecap debt here, the shylock stare-down there, the goombah getaway . . . all the stuff.

Share and share alike.

Now that we are older, we still share, and we retell the tales of our youth, but this time we take credit for each others' exploits.

You see, the statute of limitations on certain things never lapses, and if a friend can protect a friend from the ramifications of certain youthful indiscretions by taking the blame in his place, so be it.

The fun part is it's all hearsay, and just because someone heard you confess doesn't mean you actually did, and boy, is it hard to get hard evidence beyond the hearsay for a forty-year-old case . . . especially when you didn't do it.

———◆———

Judge not lest ye be judged.

And take everything the cops tell you with a grain of salt.

If your gut tells you that your buddy Tony would never give you up, don't believe the cop who says he did.

A rat isn't a rat until you know he's a rat.

Slander is a horrible crime.

Which is not to say that you should take unnecessary risks.

Let him keep his good name.

His life, well, that's another matter.

One can't be too careful.

———◆———

. . . And a Word to the Wise for Nonwiseguys

*E*mbarrassment is the greatest weapon of all.

No one wants to be known as a cuckold.

No one wants to be known as a fool.

. . . and no one *ever* wants to be known as weak.

When one knows things about someone along these lines, one keeps one's mouth shut because a weapon is always more persuasive if it is still in the holster.

People in this thing of ours are funny.

They are like everyone else.

Nobody remembers that so-and-so was sent away for credit card fraud or tax evasion or pandering.

Those are civilian concerns.

For wiseguys it's the plain embarrassment of getting caught and being made to do the time, for what, who cares?

. . . and if you were in their place, would you?

So keep your mouth shut, take everything you read with a grain of salt, add a spoonful of sugar to your homemade marinara, support your neighborhood business, and keep your nose out of other people's business.

Even if you're not a wiseguy, try to be wise.

Epilogue

One day I went back to the little hole-in-the-wall restaurant, but it was closed.

A sign read—COMING SOON: DUNKIN' DONUTS.

So goes the neighborhood.

Acknowledgments

Back in grammar school I was introduced to the lighter side of mob life through Jimmy Breslin's masterpiece, *The Gang That Couldn't Shoot Straight*, which was soon followed in my reading repertoire by *The Valachi Papers* by Peter Maas, *Honor Thy Father* by Gay Talese, and, of course, *The Godfather* by Mario Puzo.

Since that time it has been my great good fortune to have also been exposed to the works of (in no particular order) Nicholas Pileggi, Robert Daley, Harvey Aronson, Donald Goddard, Bill Bonanno, Joe Pistone, Sam Giancana, Allen C. Kupfer, Joseph R. Gannascoli, Clint Willis, Frederic Dannen, "Joey," David Fisher, George Anastasia, Ernest Volkman, Loren Estleman, Max A. Collins, Jerry Capeci, Joseph F. O'Brien, Philip Carlo, David Chase, Francis Coppola, Martin Scorsese, Sidney Lumet, T. J. English, and many folks whose names have not entered the public arena (and would like to keep it that way).

And also thanks to my father, who instilled in me a love of reading and the necessity of an awareness of what's going on around me; my editor, Lane Butler; my agent, Frank Weimann; my occasional partner in crime, Jim Fallone; my loving wife and proofreader, Donna; and the long-suffering Minx the three-legged wonder cat.

Any lapses in taste or faults of fact, I plead the fifth.

To parody is human.

To forgive divine.